THE GOSPEL OF THOMAS

APOCRYPHAL WITH COPTIC INTERLINEAR

COMMENTED BY: *Ana Méndez Ferrell, Simón Aquino, Ana Louceiro Plattner & Lorenza Méndez*

VOICE OF THE LIGHT
MINISTRIES

THE GOSPEL OF THOMAS
APOCRYPHAL WITH COPTIC INTERLINEAR

1° English Edition 2023, Commented by: Ana Méndez Ferrell,
Simón Aquino, Ana Louceiro Plattner & Lorenza Méndez.

Published by: Voice of the Light Ministries / United States of America
Telephone: +1.904.834.2447
Category: Kingdom
Cover Design: Ana Méndez Ferrell
Layout: Andrea Jaramillo

All biblical references have been extracted from New King James Version and, in some cases translated from the Amplified Bible. We also used a direct translation from the Textual Bible.

Printed in the United States and Colombia.

www.voiceofthelight.com
VOTL - P.O. Box 3418 Ponte Vedra, Florida, 32004 / U.S.A.

ISBN: 978-1-944681-61-6

INDEX

INDEX

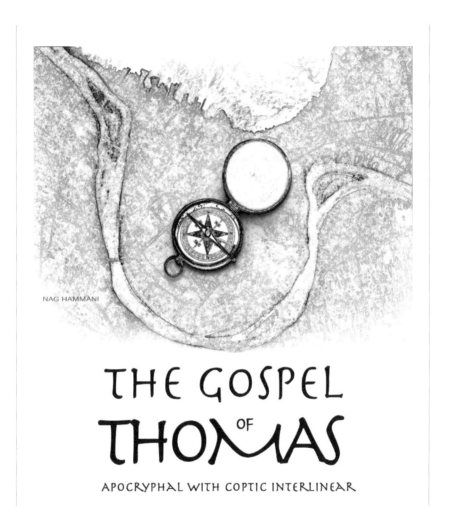

NAG HAMMANI

THE GOSPEL
THOⲘⲀS OF

APOCRYPHAL WITH COPTIC INTERLINEAR

COMMENTED BY: *Ana Méndez Ferrell, Simón Aquino, Ana Louceiro Plattner & Lorenza Méndez*

In sharing this precious document, we do so to pass on its spiritual richness.

In no way do we wish to make it equal to the Bible, which is our torch and anchor.

The Gospel of Thomas was one of the most extraordinary discoveries of the XX century.

The document was virtually unknown and lost throughout history until 1945. Before, it was known to have existed only by name.

The Gospel of Thomas was found entirely intact in the cave of Nag-Hammadi. Many call it the fifth Gospel due to the number of verses analogous to the synoptic gospels of Matthew, Mark, and Luke.

In the second century, Irenaeus, Bishop of Lyons, referred to the Gospel of Thomas in his work Against Heresies and made it a part of his assertions against Gnosticism.

The category was tacitly assumed among academics even after the discovery of the text in 1945, solely due to the phrase: written by Irenaeus.

It was not until decades later, following the gospel's subsequent analysis and translation, together with other texts found at Nag Hammadi, that scholars concluded that it was wrong to categorize the entire compendium discovered as Gnostic.

In this regard, Marvin Meyer and Elaine H. Pagels comment: "Isn't it misleading to classify these texts as Gnostic? Given their variety, we now understand that we are unfamiliar with a wide range of early Christian traditions because the bishops (Church Fathers) tried to delegitimize any viewpoints that differed from their own arguments[1]."

Therefore, recovering this gospel implies removing it from the Gnostic category, which it has been confined to by Irenaeus since the year 180.

Out of all the books found in the Nag Hammadi cave, none has attracted more attention than the Gospel of Thomas, which unlike the other gospels, is a collection of the sayings of Jesuss.

The book has 114 sayings and no chronological narrative. It does not mention the miracles, the Passion, or any of the stories of Jesus' life. It only

---

1   "Instead of referring to all the texts found at Nag Hammadi as a corporate collection, scholars today prefer to analyze them as unique and unassociated or relate them to Jewish, Christian, or pagan sources rather than assume that all these texts deviate from the mainstream of early Christianity. In this way, we open a broader spectrum to consider and understand the different sources of early Christianity. Instead of discriminating by simple assumptions that something is either orthodox or Gnostic, many scholars working on the Coptic texts now research under old and new evidence to pose new questions. For example, many of us are discussing questions such as: Is it not misleading to classify these texts as Gnostic? Given their variety, we now understand that there is a wide range of traditions of early Christianity of which we are unfamiliar because the bishops (Church Fathers) sought to delegitimize views that differed from their own personal arguments." (Meyer, 2009)

speaks of the words that proceeded out of his mouth.

Perhaps alluding to the 'private' quality of the dialogues or maxims, Thomas refers to them as: "The secret sayings that the living Jesus spoke."

Clement of Alexandria quotes the Gospel of Thomas without naming its source.

The text in question is proverb no. 2, which reads:

"Jesus said:

'He who seeks let him not cease seeking until he finds; and when he finds he will be troubled, and when he is troubled, he will be amazed, and he will reign over the All and attain rest.'"

This proves that the book, in its primitive form, already existed in

190 A.D., the date of the composition of "Stromata" ("Remedies"), the book which contains said quotation.

However, there is evidence that Thomas' Gospel may have been the earliest (indeed, his original version is earlier than 100 A.D.). At least, among the documents preserved today, it is the one that most accurately records the words spoken by the historical Jesus without any mythical-legendary additions.

Throughout this commentary, we will notice that many of the sayings are completely anti-Gnostic, and none promote any Gnostic teachings.s.

ABOUT THOMAS

One of the twelve apostles, Thomas, owes his fame to his questions and doubts. He says: "Unless I see the nail marks in his hands and put my finger where the nails were, and put my hand into his side, I will not believe." (John 20:25).

Thomas was a thinker, an analyst, a man who could reflect on deep things. That is why Jesus takes him aside to speak to him about things that would be impossible for a simple-minded person to understand. We often overlook the fact that Thomas, above all, is the first one who, when faced with the mystery of the wounds of the risen Christ, gave Jesus his proper title, confessing his faith in Jesus by saying, "My Lord and my God!" (John 20: 28)

Thomas evangelized the south of India, where he is considered the founder of the Indian Church in Malankara, arriving in 52 AD and later suffering martyrdom in 72 AD. His tomb is located in this country, in the Basilica of St. Thomas, in Chennai. Thus, he is attributed with this apocryphal gospel.

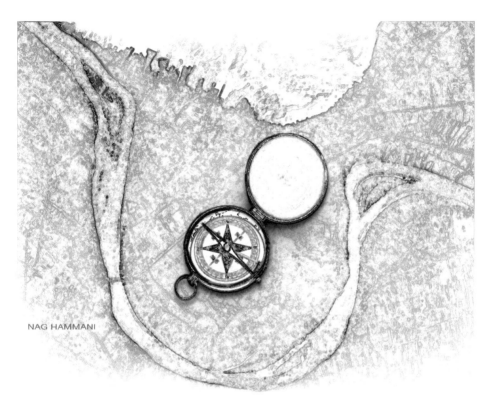

NAG HAMMANI

THE GOSPEL OF THOMAS

FOREWORD

ΝΑΕΙ	ΝΕ	Ν̅·ϢΑΧΕ	ΕΘΗΠ'	ΕΝΤΑ·Ι̅C̅	ΕΤ·ΟΝ2
These	are	the-words	()-hidden,	which-*JS01*	who-lives
·ΧΟ·ΟΥ		ΑΥⲰ	ΑϤ·C2ΑΙCΟΥ		Ν̅ϬΙ·ΔΙΔΥΜΟC
-spoke(them),		and	he-wrote-them,		viz-Didymos
ΪΟΥΔΑC	ΘⲰΜΑC		ΑΥⲰ	ΠΕΧΑ·Ϥ'	ΧΕ	ΠΕ-
Judas	Thomas,					

THE GOSPEL
THO of MAS

APOCRYPHAL WITH COPTIC INTERLINEAR

SAYINGS

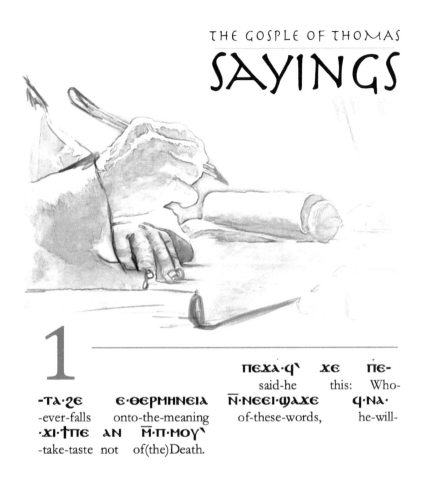

1

ⲡⲉⲝⲁ·ϥ` ⲝⲉ ⲡⲉ-
said-he this: Who-

-ⲧⲁ·ⲍⲉ ⲉ·ⲑⲉⲣⲙⲏⲛⲉⲓⲁ ⲛ̄·ⲛⲉⲉⲓ·ⲱⲁⲝⲉ ϥ·ⲛⲁ·
-ever-falls onto-the-meaning of-these-words, he-will-

·ⲝⲓ·ⲧⲡⲉ ⲁⲛ ⲙ̄·ⲡ·ⲙⲟⲩ`
-take-taste not of(the)Death.

These are the secret sayings that the living Jesus spoke and which Didymos Judas Thomas wrote down. He who finds the interpretation to these sayings shall not find death.

INTERPRETATION:

The Apostle Paul also speaks of a hidden or secret wisdom that only the mature can understand.

Thomas was one of those thinkers to whom Jesus could speak profound sayings.

> **1 Corinthians 2:6-7**
> "However, we speak wisdom among those who are mature, yet not the wisdom of this age, nor of the rulers of this age, who are coming to nothing. But we speak the wisdom of God in a mystery, the hidden wisdom which God ordained before the ages for our glory."

Jesus shared the proper interpretation of His Word with His disciples, who truly believed in Him and for which they would not see death.

> **Luke 8:10**
> "And he said, Unto you, it is given to know the mysteries of the kingdom of God: but to others in parables; that seeing they might not see, and hearing they might not understand."

Thomas is by no means implying salvation comes by understanding verses, but throughout the writing, to know Him is to believe in Him and His life within the believer.

2

ⲡⲉⲭⲉ·ⲓ̅ⲥ̅ <> ⲙ̅ⲛ̅ⲧⲣⲉϥ·ˋ
Said Jesus   (this) Let-not-him-

·ⲗⲟ   ⲛ̅ϭⲓ·ⲡⲉⲧ·ˋ·ϣⲓⲛⲉ   ⲉϥ·ˋ·ϣⲓⲛⲉ   ϣⲁⲛⲧⲉϥ·ˋ
-stop,   viz-he-who-\ -seek,   as-he-\ -seek,   until-he-

·ϭⲓⲛⲉ   ⲁⲩⲱ   ϩⲟⲧⲁⲛˋ   ⲉϥ·ϣⲁⲛ·ϭⲓⲛⲉ   ϥ·ⲛⲁ·
-find,   > and   when   he-should-find,   he-will-

·ϣⲧⲣ̅ⲧⲣ̅   ⲁⲩⲱ   ⲉϥ·ϣⲁⲛ·ˋ·ϣⲧⲟⲣⲧⲣ̅   ϥ·ⲛⲁ·ⲣ̅·
-be-troubled,   > and   if-he-should \be-troubled,   he-will-become-

(left-half of line is blank)   ·ϣⲡⲏⲣⲉ   ⲁⲩⲱ   ϥ·ⲛⲁ·ⲣ̅·
    amazed,   > and he-will-become-

·ⲣ̅ⲣⲟ   ⲉⲭⲙ̅·ⲡ·ⲧⲏⲣ·ϥ   ⲡⲉⲭⲉ·ⲓ̅ⲥ̅   ⲭⲉ   ⲉⲩ·ϣⲁ·
-king   over-the-All.

Jesus said, "Let him who seeks continue seeking until he finds. When he finds, he will become troubled. When he becomes troubled, he will be astonished, and he will rule over the all."

INTERPRETATION:

Jesus encourages us to seek the Kingdom of God.

Matthew 6:33
"But seek first the kingdom of God and His righteousness, and all these things shall be added unto you."

The Kingdom of God comprises mysteries and a reality that is not of this world. We marvel when we encounter these revelations, but some revelations shake all our natural and worldly thinking and therefore trouble us. It is only by overcoming our carnal way of thinking that we can reign over all things.

3

ⲡⲉⲝⲉ·ⲓ̄ⲥ̄ ⲝⲉ ⲉⲩ·ⳋⲁ·
Said Jesus this: If-they-should-

·ⲭⲟ·ⲟⲥ ⲛⲏ·ⲧⲛ̄ ⲛ̄ϭⲓ·ⲛⲉⲧ·ⲥⲱⲕ ϩⲏⲧ·ⲑⲩⲧⲛ̄
-speak to-you(pl), viz-those-who-\ -lead before\yourselves,

ⲝⲉ ⲉⲓⲥ·ϩⲏⲏⲧⲉ ⲉ·ⲧ·ⲙ̄ⲛ̄ⲧⲉⲣⲟ ϩⲛ̄·ⲧ·ⲡⲉ ⲉ-
this- " Behold, is-the-\ -kingdom in-the-sky", t-

-ⲉⲓⲉ ⲛ̄·ϩⲁⲗⲏⲧ· ·ⲛⲁ·ⲣ̄·ϣⲟⲣⲡ· ⲉⲣⲱ·ⲧⲛ̄ ⲛ̄ⲧⲉ·
-hen the-birds will-become-first before-you(pl) of-

·ⲧ·ⲡⲉ ⲉⲩ·ⳋⲁⲛ·ⲭⲟ·ⲟⲥ ⲛⲏ·ⲧⲛ̄ ⲝⲉ ⲥ·ϩⲛ̄·ⲑⲁ-
-the-sky. > If-they-should-speak to-you(pl) this- "She(is)in-the-s-

-ⲗⲁⲥⲥⲁ ⲉⲉⲓⲉ ⲛ̄·ⲧⲃⲧ· ·ⲛⲁ·ⲣ̄·ϣⲟⲣⲡ· ⲉⲣⲱ·ⲧⲛ̄
-ea", then the-fish will-become-first before-you(pl).

ⲁⲗⲗⲁ ⲧ·ⲙ̄ⲛ̄ⲧⲉⲣⲟ ⲥ·ⲙ̄·ⲡⲉⲧⲛ̄·ϩⲟⲩⲛ· ⲁⲩⲱ
Rather, the-kingdom, she(is)of-your(pl)-inner, and

ⲥ·ⲙ̄·ⲡⲉⲧⲛ̄·ⲃⲁⲗ· ϩⲟⲧⲁⲛ ⲉⲧⲉⲧⲛ̄·ⳋⲁⲛ·
she(is)of-your(pl)-eye(outer). > When you(pl)-should-

·ⲥⲟⲩⲱⲛ·ⲑⲏⲩⲧⲛ̄ ⲧⲟⲧⲉ ⲥⲉ·ⲛⲁ·ⲥⲟⲩⲱ̄·
-know-yourselves, then they-will-know-

·ⲑⲛⲉ ⲁⲩⲱ ⲧⲉⲧⲛⲁ·ⲉⲓⲙⲉ ⲝⲉ ⲛ̄·ⲧⲱ·ⲧⲛ̄ ⲡⲉ
-you(pl), and you(pl)-will-realize that you(pl) are

ⲛ̄·ⳋⲏⲣⲉ ⲙ̄·ⲡ·ⲉⲓⲱⲧ· ⲉⲧ·ⲟⲛϩ ⲉϣⲱⲡⲉ ⲇⲉ
the-sons of-the-father who-lives. > If, hwvr,

ⲧⲉⲧⲛⲁ·ⲥⲟⲩⲱⲛ·ⲑⲏⲩⲧⲛ̄ ⲁⲛ ⲉⲉⲓⲉ ⲧⲉⲧⲛ̄·
you(pl)-will-know-yourselves not, then you(pl)-

·ϣⲟⲟⲡ· ϩⲛ̄·ⲟⲩ·ⲙⲛ̄ⲧ·ϩⲏⲕⲉ ⲁⲩⲱ ⲛ̄·ⲧⲱ·ⲧⲛ̄
-exist in(a)poverty, and you(pl)

ⲡⲉ ⲧ·ⲙⲛ̄ⲧ·ϩⲏⲕⲉ
(are) the-poverty.

Jesus said, "If those who lead you say to you, 'See, the kingdom is in the sky,' then the birds of the sky will precede you. If they say to you, 'It is in the sea,' then the fish will precede you. Rather, the kingdom is inside of you, and it is outside of you. When you come to know yourselves, then you will become known, and you will realize that it is you who are the sons of the living father. But if you will not know yourselves, you dwell in poverty and it is you who are that poverty."

INTERPRETATION:

Jesus spoke of his Kingdom, which is in our midst.

> **Luke 17:20-21**
> "Now when He was asked by the Pharisees when the kingdom of God would come, He answered them and said, "The kingdom of God does not come with observation; nor will they say, 'See here!' or 'See there!' For indeed, the kingdom of God is within you."

Not living for and in God's Kingdom, knowing our nature as God's sons and as the spouse of the Lamb, leads to living in this existence's poverty and being ourselves that very poverty.

It is within us that the glorious unity of the Spirit of God and the spirit of man takes place, which leads us to know Christ and ourselves as sons of God, with the privileges implied.

4

πεxε·ιc
Said Jesus

πε   τ·мν̄τ·2нкε   πεxε·ιc <> q·на·хнаγ аν
(are)   the-poverty.   > *Said-*JS04* (this) He-will-delay not,

ν̄ό1·π·ρωмε   ν̄·2λλο   2ν̄·νεq·200γ   ε·хνε·
viz-the-man   of-oldness   in-his-days,   to-ask-

·0γ·к0γε1   ν̄·ϣηρε·ϣнм   εq·2ν̄·сαϣq
-a-little   small-child,   he-being-of-seven

ν̄·200γ   ετβε·π·топос   м̄·π·ωн2   аγω
days,   about-the-place   of(the)Life,   and

q·на·ωн2   xε 0γν̄·2α2   ν̄·ϣ0рп`   ·на·ρ̄·2α-
he-will-live,   > for there-are-many   first   will-become-la-

-ε   аγω   ν̄сε·ϣωπε   0γα 0γωτ   πεxε·ιc
-st,   >   and   they(will)come-to-be one   alone.   > *Said-*JS05*

Jesus said, "The man old in days will not hesitate to ask a small child seven days old about the place of life, and he will live. For many who are first will become last, and they will become one and the same."

INTERPRETATION:

This saying is parallel to

Matthew 20:16

"So, the last will be first, and the first last. For many are called, but few chose."

He shares this in the parable of the Lord of the vineyard and his workers. Some served early, and others later. Jesus, however, begins from the principle of the oneness of the Kingdom in which we are all part of the body of Christ in the perfect unity that He had with the Father.

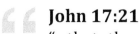

John 17:21

"...that they all may be one, as You, Father, are in Me, and I in You; that they also may be one in Us, that the world may believe that You sent Me."

On the other hand, we know that we come from God and have been chosen before the foundation of the world. (Ephesians 1:3-4) A baby is born in God's full consciousness in an almost perfect state of innocence. A state that an older person loses as they venture through this world.

5

ⲡⲉϫⲉ·ⲓ̅ⲥ̅
Said Jesus

ⲥⲟⲩⲱⲛ·ⲡⲉⲧ·ⲙ̅·ⲡ·ⲙ̅ⲧⲟ ⲙ̅·ⲡⲉⲕ·ϩⲟ ⲉⲃⲟⲗˋ
Know-what-is-in-the-presence of-your(sg)-face ( ),

ⲁⲩⲱ ⲡⲉⲑⲏⲡˋ ⲉⲣⲟ·ⲕˋ ϥ·ⲛⲁ·ϭⲱⲗⲡˋ ⲉⲃⲟⲗ
and what-is-hidden to-you(sg), ()will-be-revealed forth

ⲛⲁ·ⲕˋ ⲙⲛ̅·ⲗⲁⲁⲩ ⲅⲁⲣ ⲉϥ·ϩⲏⲡˋ ⲉϥ·ⲛⲁ·ⲟⲩⲱⲛϩ
to-you(sg), > (for) no-thing, (---), being-hidden ()will-appear

ⲉⲃⲟⲗ ⲁⲛ
forth not.

Jesus said, "Recognize what is in your sight, and that which is hidden from you will become plain to you, for there is nothing hidden which will not become manifest. nor buried that [will not be raised]."

This saying is parallel to **Mark 4:22**

> "For there is nothing hidden which will not be revealed, nor has anything been kept secret but that it should come to light."

Jesus is not speaking so much here about sins or hidden intentions but about revelations in the dimensions of the Kingdom that lie behind apparent things.

He is also referring to the resurrection nature that manifests itself through us.

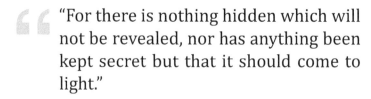

6

ПЄХЄ·ІC	ХЄ	М̅П̅Р̅·ХЄ·6Оλ	λY-
Said Jesus	this:	Do-not-tell-lies,	> an-

-ω	ПЄТЄТМ̅·МОCТЄ	М̅·МО·ϥ`	М̅П̅Р̅·λ·λϥ	ХЄ
-d	that-which-you(pl)-hate	(it(m)),	do-not-do-it(m),	> for

CЄ·6ОλП`	ТНР·ОY	ЄВОλ	М̅·ПЄ·МТО	ЄВОλ
they-are-revealed,	all-of-them,	forth,	in-the-presence	( )

N̅·Т·ПЄ	МN̅·λλλY	ГλР	ЄϥП·2НП`	Єϥ·Nλ·ОY-
of-the-sky,	>(for) no-thing,	(---),	()hidden	()may-ap-

-ωN2	ЄВОλ	λN	λYω	МN̅·λλλY	Єϥ·2ОВC̅	ЄY·
-pear	forth	not,	> and	nothing	()covered	they-

·Nλ·6ω	ОYЄϣN̅·6ОλП·ϥ`
-will-remain	without-revealing-it(m).

His disciples questioned him and said to him, "Do you want us to fast? How shall we pray? Shall we give alms? What diet shall we observe?"

Jesus said, "Do not lie, and do not do what you hate, for all things are plain in the sight of heaven. For nothing hidden will not become manifest, and nothing covered will remain without being uncovered.

INTERPRETATION:

In this saying, Jesus speaks against hypocrisy, extensively practiced by the Pharisees and today by religious people. They did and do things out of obligation and not out of their heart's desire. Even while hating to give offerings, fast, or pray, they still do so to comply with a religious system. All this is abominable to God, who sees our heart's intentions.

The whole of chapter 6 of Matthew amplifies this saying of Jesus.

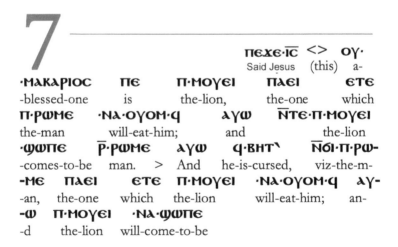

7

			ΠΕΧΕ·ΙC	<>	ΟΥ·
			Said Jesus	(this)	a-
·ΜΑΚΑΡΙΟC	ΠΕ	Π·ΜΟΥΕΙ	ΠΑΕΙ		ΕΤΕ
-blessed-one	is	the-lion,	the-one		which
Π·ΡШΜΕ	·ΝΑ·ΟΥΟΜ·Ϥ		ΑΥШ	ΝΤΕ·Π·ΜΟΥΕΙ	
the-man	will-eat-him;		and	the-lion	
·ШШΠΕ	Ρ·ΡШΜΕ	ΑΥШ	Ϥ·ΒΗΤˋ	ΝϬΙ·Π·ΡШ-	
-comes-to-be	man.	> And	he-is-cursed,	viz-the-m-	
-ΜΕ	ΠΑΕΙ	ΕΤΕ	Π·ΜΟΥΕΙ	·ΝΑ·ΟΥΟΜ·Ϥ	ΑΥ-
-an,	the-one	which	the-lion	will-eat-him;	an-
-Ш	Π·ΜΟΥΕΙ	·ΝΑ·ШШΠΕ			
-d	the-lion	will-come-to-be			

Jesus said, "Blessed is the lion which becomes man when consumed by man; and cursed is the man whom the lion consumes, and the lion becomes man."

One can symbolically apply the term lion to this world's system. There are several instances where we see Kingdoms represented by beasts as described by the prophet Daniel.

When a righteous man crucifies this world to himself (the man eats the lion), transforming him into righteousness, thus blessing the world (the lion).

When the system of this world (the lion) devours the wicked, it is cursed by his very iniquity.

This world's system takes on the form of the consciousness of men consumed by it.

> Peter also refers to the devil who, like a roaring lion, seeks whom he may devour (1 Peter 5:8), which applies to the second part of the saying: Cursed is the man whom the devil devours since he will take possession of everything that person is. This way, the devil makes himself visible and strips his prey of everything.

Another interpretation can be:

> That man, superior to the lion, represents life in the spirit. The lion, inferior to man, depicts life in the flesh. When the life of the Spirit absorbs (consumes) the life of the flesh, everything we do in our humanity becomes spiritual (pray, fast, give.)

However, when a carnal life absorbs or eliminates the spiritual life, the spiritual life ceases, and the carnal one succeeds.

8

ⲁⲩⲱ ⲡⲉ-
> And sa-
-ϫⲁ·ϥ ϫⲉ ⲉ·ⲡ·ⲣⲱⲙⲉ ·ⲧⲛ̄ⲧⲱⲛ ⲁ·ⲩ·ⲟⲩⲱϩⲉ
-id-he this: does-the-man compare to-a-fisherman
ⲣ̄·ⲣⲙ·ⲛ̄·ϩⲏⲧ` ⲡⲁⲉⲓ ⲛ̄ⲧⲁϩ·ⲛⲟⲩϫⲉ ⲛ̄·ⲧⲉϥ·ⲁ-
wise, the-one who-cast his-n-
-ⲃⲱ ⲉ·ⲑⲁⲗⲁⲥⲥⲁ ⲁϥ·ⲥⲱⲕ ⲙ̄·ⲙⲟ·ⲥ ⲉ·ϩⲣⲁï
-et to-the-sea; he-drew her up
ϩⲛ̄·ⲑⲁⲗⲁⲥⲥⲁ ⲉⲥ·ⲙⲉϩ ⲛ̄·ⲧⲃⲧ` ⲛ̄·ⲕⲟⲩⲉⲓ ⲛ̄·
from-the-sea, she-being-full of-fish, little-ones from-
·ϩⲣⲁï ⲛ̄·ϩⲏⲧ·ⲟⲩ ⲁϥ·ϩⲉ ⲁ·ⲩ·ⲛⲟϭ ⲛ̄·ⲧⲃ̄ⲧ ⲉ·ⲛⲁ-
-below; > among-them he-fell upon-a-great fish, -
-ⲛⲟⲩ·ϥ` ⲛ̄ϭⲓ·ⲡ·ⲟⲩⲱϩⲉ ⲣ̄·ⲣⲙ·ⲛ̄·ϩⲏⲧ` ⲁϥ·ⲛⲟⲩ-
-good(), viz-the-fisherman wise; > did-he-ca-
-ϫⲉ ⲛ̄·ⲛ̄·ⲕⲟⲩⲉⲓ ⲧⲏⲣ·ⲟⲩ ⲛ̄·ⲧⲃⲧ` ⲉⲃⲟⲗ ⲉ[ⲡ·ⲉ]-
-st the-little-ones all-of-them fish back (d-
-ⲥⲏⲧ` ⲉ·ⲑⲁⲗⲁⲥⲥⲁ ⲁϥ·ⲥⲱⲧⲡ` ⲙ̄·ⲡ·ⲛⲟϭ ⲛ̄·
-own) to-the-sea; did-he-choose the-great -
·ⲧⲃ̄ⲧ ⲭⲱⲣⲓⲥ·ϩⲓⲥⲉ ⲡⲉⲧⲉ·ⲟⲩⲛ̄·ⲙⲁⲁϫⲉ ⲙ̄·ⲙⲟ·ϥ
-fish without-trouble. > He-who-has-ear of-him
ⲉ·ⲥⲱⲧⲙ̄ ⲙⲁⲣⲉϥ·`·ⲥⲱⲧⲙ̄
to-listen, let-him- \ -listen.

And he said, "The man is like a wise fisherman who cast his net into the sea and drew it up from the sea full of small fish. Among them the wise fisherman found a fine large fish. He threw all the small fish back into the sea and chose the large fish without difficulty. Whoever has ears to hear, let him hear."

INTERPRETATION:

This saying is parallel to

 Matthew 13:47-48

"Again, the Kingdom of Heaven is like a dragnet that was cast into the sea and gathered some of every kind; which, when it was full, they drew to shore; and they sat down and gathered the good into vessels, but threw the bad away."

This speaks to us of God's choice for his faithful disciples, who are hearers of His Word and whose hearts are receptive and humble to follow his commandments.

9

ⲡⲉϫⲉ·ⲓ̅ⲥ̅ ⲉⲓⲥ·ϩⲏ-
Said Jesus Beho-

-ⲏⲧⲉˋ ⲁϥ·ⲉⲓ ⲉⲃⲟⲗ ⲛ̅ϭⲓ·ⲡⲉⲧ·ˋ·ⲥⲓⲧⲉ ϥ·ⲙⲉϩ·ⲧⲟⲟⲧ·ϥ̅
-ld, he-came out, viz-he-who-\-sows; he-fills-his-hand,

ⲁϥ·ⲛⲟⲩϫⲉ ⲁ·ϩⲟⲉⲓⲛⲉ ⲙⲉⲛ ·ϩⲉ ⲉⲝⲛ̅·ⲧⲉ·ϩⲓⲏˋ
he-cast; > did-some, indeed, fall onto-the-road;

ⲁⲩ·ⲉⲓ ⲛ̅ϭⲓ·ⲛ̅·ϩⲁⲗⲁⲧⲉ ⲁⲩ·ⲕⲁⲧϥ·ⲟⲩ ϩⲛ̅·ⲕⲟⲟⲩⲉ
they-came, viz-the-birds; they-gathered-them; > some-others,

ⲁⲩ·ϩⲉ ⲉⲝⲛ̅·ⲧ·ⲡⲉⲧⲣⲁ ⲁⲩⲱ ⲙ̅ⲡⲟⲩ·ϫⲉ·ⲛⲟⲩⲛⲉ
they-fell onto-the-rock, and did-not()send-roots

ⲉ·ⲡ·ⲉⲥⲏⲧˋ ⲉ·ⲡ·ⲕⲁϩ ⲁⲩⲱ ⲙ̅ⲡⲟⲩ·ⲧⲉⲩⲉ·ϩⲙ̅ⲥ̅ ⲉ·ϩ-
(down) to-the-earth, and did-not()send-ears ris-

-ⲣⲁⲓ̈ ⲉ·ⲧ·ⲡⲉ ⲁⲩⲱ ϩⲛ̅·ⲕⲟⲟⲩⲉ ⲁⲩ·ϩⲉ ⲉⲝⲛ̅·ⲛ̅·ϣⲟ̅ -
-ing to-the-sky. > And some-others, they-fell onto-thorn-

-ⲧⲉ ⲁⲩ·ⲱϭⲧˋ ⲙ̅·ⲡⲉ·ϭⲣⲟϭ ⲁⲩⲱ ⲁ·ⲡ·ϥⲛ̅ⲧ ·ⲟⲩⲟⲙ·ⲟⲩ
-s; they-choked the-seed, and did-the-worm eat-them;

ⲁⲩⲱ ⲁ·ϩⲛ̅·ⲕⲟⲟⲩⲉ ·ϩⲉ ⲉⲝⲛ̅·ⲡ·ⲕⲁϩ ⲉⲧ·ⲛⲁⲛⲟⲩ·ϥˋ
and did-some-others fall upon-the-earth which-was-good(),

ⲁⲩⲱ ⲁϥ·ϯ·ⲕⲁⲣⲡⲟⲥ ⲉ·ϩⲣⲁⲓ̈ ⲉ·ⲧ·ⲡⲉ ⲉ·ⲛⲁⲛⲟⲩ·ϥˋ ⲁϥ·
and it(m)-gave-fruit up to-the-sky good(); did-he-

·ⲉⲓ ⲛ̅·ⲥⲉ ⲉ·ⲥⲟⲧⲉ ⲁⲩⲱ ϣⲉ·ϫⲟⲩⲱⲧˋ ⲉ·ⲥⲟⲧⲉ
-come 60 per-measure, and 120 per-measure.

Jesus said, "Now the Sower went out, took a handful (of seeds), and scattered them. Some fell on the road; the birds came and gathered them up. Others fell on rock, did not take root in the soil, and did not produce ears. And others fell on thorns; they choked the seed(s) and worms ate them. And others fell on the good soil and it produced good fruit: it bore sixty per measure and a hundred and twenty per measure."

INTERPRETATION:

The saying is parallel to

> ## Matthew 13:3-9
>
> "Then He spoke many things to them in parables, saying: "Behold, a sower went out to sow. And as he sowed, some seed fell by the wayside; and the birds came and devoured them. Some fell on stony places, where they did not have much earth; and they immediately sprang up because they had no depth of earth. But when the sun was up they were scorched, and because they had no root they withered away. And some fell among thorns, an the thorns sprang up and choked them. But others fell on good ground and yielded a crop: some a hundredfold, some sixty, some thirty. He who has ears to hear, let him hear!"

10

ΠΕΧΕ·ΙC	ΧΕ	ΛΕΙ·ΝΟΥΧΕ	Ν·ΟΥ·ΚⲰ2Τ`	ΕΧΝ·
Said Jesus	this:	I-have-cast	(a)fire	upon-
·Π·ΚΟCΜΟC	ΛΥⲰ	ΕΙC·2ΗΗΤΕ	†·ΛΡΕ2	ΕΡΟ·ϥ`
-the-world,	and	behold,	I-watch	over-him
ⲰΛΝΤΕϥ·ΧΕΡΟ	ΠΕΧΕ·ΙC	ΧΕ	ΤΕΕΙ·ΠΕ	·ΝΛ·Ρ·ΠΛ-
until-he-burns.				

Jesus said, "I have cast fire upon the world, and see, I am guarding it until it blazes."

INTERPRETATION:

Fire has a two-fold meaning. On the one hand, it is the fire of the Spirit, the promise fulfilled at Pentecost. It is a fire that burns our personal vision, revealing our true nature. This fire is like God's flaming sword that cuts through our attachments to this world's system.

Matthew 3:11
John the Baptist said: "I indeed baptize you with water unto repentance, but He who is coming after me is mightier than I, whose sandals I am not worthy to carry. He will baptize you with the Holy Spirit and fire."

Fire is also a symbol of justice, purification, and judgment.

The passage from **Matthew 3:12** concludes by saying:

"His winnowing fan is in His hand, and He will thoroughly clean out His threshing floor, and gather His wheat into the barn; but He will burn up the chaff with unquenchable fire.").

We find another example along the same lines in

2 Samuel 22:9 and 13-15
"Smoke went up from His nostrils, and devouring fire from His mouth; Coals were kindled by it. From the brightness before Him coals of fire were kindled.

The Lord thundered from heaven, and the Most High uttered His voice. He sent arrows and scattered them; Lightning bolts and vanquished them."

When righteousness was fulfilled through Christ's life, death, and resurrection, the religious system that Israel was transformed into, misaligned from God, was destroyed by fire. That occurred in 70AD when Jerusalem and the temple were destroyed by fire.

11

ⲠⲈⲭⲈ·ⲒⲤ ⲭⲈ ⲦⲈⲈⲒ·ⲠⲈ ·ⲚⲀ·Ⲣ̄·ⲠⲀ-
Said Jesus this: This-heaven will-pass-

-ⲣⲀⲅⲈ ⲀⲨⲱ ⲦⲈⲦ·Ⲛ̄·Ⲧ·ⲠⲈ Ⲙ̄·ⲘⲞ·Ⲥ ·ⲚⲀ·Ⲣ̄·ⲠⲀⲣⲀⲅⲈ
-away, and she-who-is-above her will-pass-away,

ⲀⲨⲱ ⲚⲈⲦ·ⲘⲞⲞⲨⲦ ⲤⲈ·ⲞⲚⲨ ⲀⲚ ⲀⲨⲱ ⲚⲈⲦ·ⲞⲚⲨ
and those-who-are-dead, they-live not, and those-who-live,

ⲤⲈ·ⲚⲀ·ⲘⲞⲨ ⲀⲚ Ⲛ̄·ⲨⲞⲞⲨ ⲚⲈ·ⲦⲈⲦⲚ̄·ⲞⲨⲱⲘ`
they-will-die not. > The-days you(pl)-were-eating

Ⲙ̄·ⲠⲈⲦ·ⲘⲞⲞⲨⲦ` ⲚⲈ·ⲦⲈⲦⲚ̄·ⲈⲒⲠⲈ Ⲙ̄·ⲘⲞ·Ⳡ Ⲙ̄·ⲠⲈ-
what-is-dead, you(pl)-were-making it(m) that-

-Ⲧ·ⲞⲚⲨ ⲨⲞⲦⲀⲚ ⲈⲦⲈⲦⲚ̄·ⲱⲀⲚ·ⲱⲰⲠⲈ ⲨⲘ̄·Ⲡ·ⲞⲨ-
-which-lives; when you(pl)-should-come-to-be in-the-l-

-ⲞⲈⲒⲚ ⲞⲨ ⲠⲈ ⲦⲈⲦⲚⲀ·Ⲁ·Ⳡ ⲨⲘ̄·ⲪⲞⲞⲨ ⲈⲦⲈⲦⲚ̄·
-ight, what is (it) you(pl)-will-do()? > On-the-day you(pl)-

·Ⲟ Ⲛ̄·ⲞⲨⲀ ⲀⲦⲈⲦⲚ̄·ⲈⲒⲠⲈ Ⲙ̄·Ⲡ·ⲤⲚⲀⲨ ⲨⲞⲦⲀⲚ ⲀⲈ
-were one, you(pl)-made the-two; when, hwvr,

ⲈⲦⲈⲦⲚ̄·ⲱⲀ·ⲱⲰⲠⲈ Ⲛ̄·ⲤⲚⲀⲨ` ⲞⲨ ⲠⲈ ⲈⲦⲈ-
you(pl)-should-come-to-be two, what is (it) which

-ⲦⲚ̄·ⲚⲀ·Ⲁ·Ⳡ`
-you(pl)will-do()?

Jesus said, "This heaven will pass away, and the one above it will pass away. The dead are not alive, and the living will not die. In the days when you consumed what is dead, you made it what is alive. When you come to dwell in the light, what will you do? On the day when you were one you became two. But when you become two, what will you do?"

INTERPRETATION:

Jesus came to destroy the works of the devil and the celestial spheres from which the devil operates.

Ephesians 6:12
"For we do not wrestle against flesh and blood, but against principalities, against powers, against the rulers of [a]the darkness of this age, against spiritual hosts of wickedness in the heavenly places."

These heavenly Regions of wickedness are made up of various layers such as Babylon, "the spiritual city that reigns over the kings of the earth" **(Revelation 17:18)**, and the false Rachia made up of the stars and constellations ruled by the forces of evil.

Once Jesus Christ sat on the throne as King of kings, we saw a radical change in how God's heavens operate and are shaped. Heaven is not the same with an empty throne as with the King seated on it.

The phrase "And the dead are not alive and the living shall not die," refers to the spiritual condition of souls.

> **John 5:24**
> "Most assuredly, I say to you, he who hears My word and believes in Him who sent Me has everlasting life, and shall not come into judgment, but has passed from death into life."

> **John 11:25**
> "Jesus said to her, "I am the resurrection and the life. He who believes in Me, though he may die, he shall live."

The phrase: "In the days when you ate what is dead, you transformed it to life" refers to assimilating what proceeds from this world's system, the concepts of death the world feeds from, and bringing them to the truth of life, transforming darkness with the Light of Christ in us.

The last part of the saying concerns the oneness of the Father in Light from whence we come. Upon coming to this world of darkness, our soul and spirit were separated, but by returning to the Light, we must reunify our minds and heart with the truth of the Light. Thus, by being unified within ourselves and becoming one with Jesus, we can be one with the Father and the other members of the true body of Jesus.

12

ΠΕΧΕ·Μ·ΜΑΘΗΤΗС Ν·ΙС ΧΕ ΤΝ·
Said-the-disciples to- this: we-

·СООΥΝ ΧΕ Κ·ΝΑ·ΒШΚ` Ν·ΤΟΟΤ·Ν ΝΙΜ` ΠΕ
-know that you(sg)-will-go from-our-hand. Who is-he

ΕΤ·ΝΑ·Ρ·ΝΟ6 Ε·2ΡΑΪ ΕΧШ·Ν ΠΕΧΕ·ΙС ΝΑ·Υ
who-will-become-great, up over-us? *Said-JS12 to-them

ΧΕ Π·ΜΑ ΝΤΑΤΕΤΝ·ΕΙ Μ·ΜΑΥ ΕΤΕΤΝΑ·
this: the-place you(pl)-have-come there, you(pl)-will-be-

·ΒШΚ` ШΑ·ΪΑΚШΒΟС Π·ΔΙΚΑΙΟС ΠΑΕΙ ΝΤΑ·
-going upto-Jacob the-righteous, the-one has-

·Τ·ΠΕ ΜΝ·Π·ΚΑ2 ·ШШΠΕ ΕΤΒΗΤ·q
-the-sky and-the-earth come-into-being because-of-him.

The disciples said to Jesus, "We know that you will depart from us. Who is to be our leader?" Jesus said to them, "Wherever you are, you are to go to James the righteous, for whose sake heaven and earth came into being."

INTERPRETATION:

Several sources establish that James 'the Just,' the brother of Jesus, was the Church's first leader. The Bible mentions him in Acts 15:13-21, where he gives the last word before the council of Jerusalem.

According to historical sources, Clement, bishop of Alexandria, writes:

> "The source of most of the references in the patristic literature on St. James is the 'History of the Church,' a work by Eusebius of Caesarea, written in the fourth century. It is the oldest existing source that identifies St. James as the first bishop of Jerusalem. In his first mention, Eusebius refers to the Pauline testimony of 1 Corinthians 15:5-7 by stating that Jesus "appeared to James (who was one of the Savior's brothers)." The following reference of Eusebius (2.1.5) points out that "James, who was called the brother of the Lord because he was also referred to as Joseph's son" and "[whom] the ancients surnamed Justus because of his extraordinary virtue," was "chosen" as bishop of Jerusalem at the time of Stephen's martyrdom. Immediately afterward, he quotes twice from the Hypotyposis of Clement of Alexandria (II-III century)." [1]

The mention at the end of the saying, "for whose sake the heavens and the earth came into being," in our opinion, has a broader meaning, referring to God's love for the righteous. God created the heavens and the earth to have a family for Him. These are the saints and the righteous of all ages.

---

1   https://profilbaru.com/es/Santiago_el_Justo

13

ⲡⲉⲭⲉ·ⲓ̅ⲥ̅
Said Jesus

Ⲛ̅·ⲛⲉϥ·ⲙⲁⲑⲏⲧⲏⲥ   ⲭⲉ   ·ⲧⲛ̅ⲧⲱⲛ·ⲧ`   ⲛ̅ⲧⲉⲧⲛ̅·
to-his-disciples   this: " Compare-me,   &-(you(pl))-

·ⲭⲟ·ⲟⲥ ⲛⲁ·ⲉⲓ ⲭⲉ   ⲉ·ⲉⲓⲛⲉ   ⲛ̅·ⲛⲓⲙ   ⲡⲉⲭⲁ·ϥ   ⲛⲁ·ϥ`
-speak   to-me   this-   I-resemble   whom?"   > Said-he   to-him,

ⲛ̅ϭⲓ·ⲥⲓⲙⲱⲛ·ⲡⲉⲧⲣⲟⲥ   ⲭⲉ   ⲉⲕ·ⲉⲓⲛⲉ   ⲛ̅·ⲟⲩ·ⲁⲅ`
viz-Simon-Peter,   this: "You(sg)-resemble   an-an-

-ⲅⲉⲗⲟⲥ ⲛ̅·ⲇⲓⲕⲁⲓⲟⲥ   ⲡⲉⲭⲁ·ϥ   ⲛⲁ·ϥ   ⲛ̅ϭⲓ·ⲙⲁⲑ`
-gel   righteous."   > Said-he   to-him,   viz-Mat-

-ⲑⲁⲓⲟⲥ ⲭⲉ   ⲉⲕ·ⲉⲓⲛⲉ   ⲛ̅·ⲟⲩ·ⲣⲱⲙⲉ ⲙ̅·ⲫⲓⲗⲟⲥⲟ-
-thew,   this: "You(sg)-resemble   a-man   of-philoso-

-ⲫⲟⲥ ⲛ̅·ⲣⲙ̅·ⲛ̅·ϩⲏⲧ`   ⲡⲉⲭⲁ·ϥ   ⲛⲁ·ϥ   ⲛ̅ϭⲓ·ⲑⲱⲙⲁⲥ
-phy   wise."   > Said-he   to-him,   viz-Thomas,

ⲭⲉ   ⲡ·ⲥⲁϩ ϩⲟⲗⲱⲥ ⲧⲁ·ⲧⲁⲡⲣⲟ ·ⲛⲁ·ϣⲁⲡ·ϥ`   ⲁⲛ
this: "Master,   wholly   my-mouth   will-accept()   not

ⲉⲧⲣⲁ·ⲭⲟ·ⲟⲥ ⲭⲉ   ⲉⲕ·ⲉⲓⲛⲉ   ⲛ̅·ⲛⲓⲙ`   ⲡⲉⲭⲉ·ⲓ̅ⲏ̅ⲥ̅
that-I-speak   that you(sg)-resemble   whom."   > Said-*JES1*

ⲭⲉ ⲁⲛⲟ·ⲕ` ⲡⲉⲕ·`·ⲥⲁϩ ⲁⲛ ⲉⲡⲉⲓ ⲁⲕ·ⲥⲱ ⲁⲕ·ϯϩⲉ
this: " I (am) your(sg)\master not; because you-drank, you-got-drunk

ⲉⲃⲟⲗ   ϩⲛ̅·ⲧ·ⲡⲏⲅⲏ   ⲉⲧ·ⲃⲣ̅ⲃⲣⲉ   ⲧⲁⲉⲓ   ⲁⲛⲟ·ⲕ`
out   of-the-spring   which-bubbles,   the-one   I

ⲛ̅ⲧⲁⲉⲓ·ϣⲓⲧ·ⲥ̅   ⲁⲩⲱ   ⲁϥ·ⲭⲓⲧ·ϥ̅   ⲁϥ·ⲁⲛⲁⲭⲱⲣⲉⲓ
have()measured-her;"   > And   he-took-him,   he-withdrew,

ⲁϥ·ⲭⲱ   ⲛⲁ·ϥ   ⲛ̅·ϣⲟⲙⲧ`   ⲛ̅·ϣⲁⲭⲉ   ⲛ̅ⲧⲁⲣⲉ·ⲑⲱ-
he-spoke   to-him   three   words.   > When-Tho-

-ⲙⲁⲥ ⲇⲉ ·ⲉⲓ ϣⲁ·ⲛⲉϥ·`·ϣⲃⲉⲉⲣ` ⲁⲩ·ⲭⲛⲟⲩ·ϥ` ⲭⲉ
-mas, hwvr, came   upto-his\ companions, they-asked-him   this:

ⲛ̅ⲧⲁ·ⲓ̅ⲥ̅   ·ⲭⲟ·ⲟⲥ ⲭⲉ ⲟⲩ ⲛⲁ·ⲕ`    ⲡⲉⲭⲁ·ϥ` ⲛⲁ·ⲩ ⲛ̅ϭⲓ·
Did-*JS14*   speak   () what to-you(sg)? > Said-he   to-them, viz-

·ⲑⲱⲙⲁⲥ ⲭⲉ   ⲉⲓ·ϣⲁⲛ·`·ⲭⲱ   ⲛⲏ·ⲧⲛ̅   ⲟⲩⲁ ϩⲛ̅·ⲛ̅·ϣⲁ-
-Thomas,   this: If-I-should-\-speak to-you(pl) one   of-the-wor-

-ⲭⲉ ⲛ̅ⲧⲁϥ·ⲭⲟ·ⲟⲩ   ⲛⲁ·ⲉⲓ   ⲧⲉⲧⲛⲁ·ϥⲓ·ⲱⲛⲉ   ⲛ̅ⲧⲉ-
-ds   he-has-spoken()   to-me,   you(pl)-will-take-stones   &-

-ⲧⲛ̅·ⲛⲟⲩⲭⲉ   ⲉⲣⲟ·ⲉⲓ   ⲁⲩⲱ   ⲛ̅ⲧⲉ·ⲟⲩ·ⲕⲱϩⲧ`   ·ⲉⲓ ⲉ-
-( )cast (them) at-me,   and   (will)(a)fire   come   -

-ⲃⲟⲗ ϩⲛ̅·ⲛ̅·ⲱⲛⲉ   ⲛ̅ⲥ·ⲣⲱⲕϩ`   ⲙ̅·ⲙⲱ·ⲧⲛ̅   ⲡⲉⲭⲉ·
-out   of-the-stones, &-(she-will)-burn   you(pl).   *Said-

Jesus said to his disciples, "Compare me to someone and tell me whom I am like." Simon Peter said to him, "You are like a righteous angel." Matthew said to him, "You are like a wise philosopher."

Thomas said to him, "Master, my mouth is wholly incapable of saying whom you are like." Jesus said, "I am not your (sg.) master. Because you (sg.) have drunk, you (sg.) have become intoxicated from the bubbling spring which I have caused to gush forth."

And he took him and withdrew and told him three things. When Thomas returned to his companions, they asked him, "What did Jesus say to you?" Thomas said to them, "If I tell you one of the things which he told me, you will pick up stones and throw them at me; a fire will come out of the stones and burn you up."

(Some translations leave out the three words and say: He spoke to him three words, or He said three words to him.)

INTERPRETATION:

John 15:15
Jesus is seen as John the Baptist, Elijah, Jeremiah, or other resurrected prophets. Thus, in Thomas, Simon Peter erroneously compares Jesus to an angel (a widespread belief among early Judeo-Christians). Matthew mistakenly compares him to a wise philosopher. Thomas rightly points out that comparing Jesus to anyone is impossible,

yet he addresses him as 'Teacher.' Jesus rebukes him for the title he uses because he no longer considers them servants or disciples but friends. After all, he has told them everything he heard from His Father.

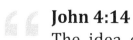

John 4:14

The idea expressed by Thomas is quite similar to that given by John. Jesus is not Thomas' master because he has drunk from the gushing wellspring that Jesus has dispensed.

John 7:37-38

John also expresses this thought: "The water I give you shall become a fountain of water springing up to eternal life."

By considering Thomas his friend, Jesus is going to reveal something to him that others at that moment could not process::

a. Possibly his divine nature. "I am the One who I Am."

b. Or, that he would be taken out of their midst.

c. Or, that they were going to kill him.

Things that later in the Gospels would lead to great confusion and pain for the disciples.

14

ΠΕΧΕ·ΙC
Said Jesus

ΝΑ·Υ ΧΕ ΕΤΕΤΝ·ϢΑΝ·Ρ·ΝΗCΤΕΥΕ ΤΕΤΝΑ·
to-them this: If-you(pl)-should-fast, you(pl)-will-

·ΧΠΟ ΝΗ·ΤΝ Ν·ΝΟΥ·ΝΟΒΕ ΑΥⲰ ΕΤΕΤΝ·ϢΑ·
-beget to-you(rselves) a-sin, > and if-you(pl)-should-

·ϢΛΗΛ CΕ·ΝΑ·Ρ·ΚΑΤΑΚΡΙΝΕ Μ·ΜⲰ·ΤΝ ΑΥⲰ
-pray, they-will-condemn you(pl), > and

ΕΤΕΤΝ·ϢΑΝ·Τ·ΕΛΕΗΜΟCΥΝΗ ΕΤΕΤΝΑ·ΕΙ·
if-you(pl)-should-give-alms, you(pl)-will-be-do-

·ΡΕ Ν·ΟΥ·ΚΑΚΟΝ Ν·ΝΕΤΜ·ΠΝΑ ΑΥⲰ ΕΤΕΤΝ·
-ing an-evil to-your(pl)-spirits, > and if-you(pl)-

·ϢΑΝ·ΒⲰΚ ΕϨΟΥΝ Ε·ΚΑϨ ·ΝΙΜ ΑΥⲰ ΝΤΕΤΜ·
-should-go in to-land -any, and ()you(pl)-

·ΜΟΟϢΕ ϨΝ·Ν·ΧⲰΡΑ ΕΥ·ϢΑ·Ρ·ΠΑΡΑΔΕΧΕ
-walk in-the-districts, if-they-should-receive

Μ·ΜⲰ·ΤΝ ΠΕΤ·ΟΥ·ΝΑ·ΚΑΑ·Ϥ ϨΑΡⲰ·ΤΝ ·ΟΥΟΜ·Ϥ
you(pl), what-they-will-put-him under-you(pl), eat-it(m);

ΝΕΤ·ϢⲰΝΕ Ν·ϨΗΤ·ΟΥ ΕΡΙ·ΘΕΡΑΠΕΥΕ Μ·ΜΟ·
those-who-are-sick among-them, heal th-

·ΟΥ ΠΕΤ·ΝΑ·ΒⲰΚ ΓΑΡ ΕϨΟΥΝ ϨΝ·ΤΕΤΝ·ΤΑ·
-em, > (for) what-will-go, (---), in ()your(pl)-mo-

·ΠΡΟ Ϥ·ΝΑ·ΧⲰϨΜ·ΤΗΥΤΝ ΑΝ ΑΛΛΑ ΠΕΤ·Ν·
-uth, it(m)-will-defile-yourselves not. Rather, what(m)-

·ΝΗΥ ΕΒΟΛ ϨΝ·ΤΕΤΝ·ΤΑΠΡΟ Ν·ΤΟ·Ϥ ΠΕ·
-comes out of-your(pl)-mouth, it(m) (is) what-

·Τ·ΝΑ·ΧΑϨΜ·ΤΗΥΤΝ
-will-defile-yourselves.

Jesus said to them, "If you fast, you will give rise to sin for yourselves; and if you pray, you will be condemned; and if you give alms, you will do harm to your spirits. When you go into any land and walk about in the districts, if they receive you, eat what they will set before you, and heal the sick among them. For what goes into your mouth will not defile you, but that which issues from your mouth—it is that which will defile you."

The Pharisees had made fasting, prayer, and offering-giving a ritualistic way of being seen by men **(Matthew 6)**. Jesus points out that it is not the external that God looks at but the internal. **Matthew 15:11**

The second part of this saying is also analogous to the Gospels in which Jesus insists that it is not that which is external that defiles a person but that which proceeds out of the heart of man.

15

ΠΕΧΕ·ΙC	ΧΕ	ϨΟΤΑΝ
Said Jesus	this:	When

ΕΤΕΤΝ·ϢΑΝ·ΝΑΥ   Ε·ΠΕΤΕ·ΜΠΟΥ·ΧΠΟ·ϥˋ
you(pl)-should-look   upon-he-who-did-not-they-beget()

ΕΒΟΛ   ϨΝ·Τ·CϨΙΜΕ   ·ΠΕϨΤ·ˋ·ΤΗΥΤΝ   ΕΧΜ·
out   of-the-woman,   prostrate\yourselves   onto-

·ΠΕΤΝ·ϨΟ   ΝΤΕΤΝ·ΟΥϢϢΤ   ΝΑ·ϥˋ   ΠΕΤ·Μ·
-your(pl)-face   &()worship   ()him -   he-who-is-

·ΜΑΥ   ΠΕ   ΠΕΤΝ·ΕΙϢΤˋ
-there   is   your(pl)-father.

Jesus said, "When you see one who was not born of woman, prostrate yourselves on your faces and worship him. That one is your father."

The verse is self-explanatory. Only the Father alone was created, but He is the author of everything.

16

ⲠⲈⲬⲈ·ⲒⲤ ⲬⲈ ⲦⲀⲬⲀ
Said Jesus this: Perhaps

ⲈⲨ·ⲘⲈⲈⲨⲈ ⲚϬⲒ·Ⲣ̄·ⲢⲰⲘⲈ ⲬⲈ ⲚⲦⲀⲈⲒ·ⲈⲒ Ⲉ·ⲚⲞⲨ-
they-are-thinking, viz-men, that I-have-come to-ca-

-ⲬⲈ Ⲛ̄·ⲞⲨ·ⲈⲒⲢⲎⲚⲎ ⲈⲬⲘ̄·Ⲡ·ⲔⲞⲤⲘⲞⲤ ⲀⲨⲰ
-st (a)peace onto-the-world, > and

ⲤⲈ·ⲤⲞⲞⲨⲚ ⲀⲚ ⲬⲈ ⲚⲦⲀⲈⲒ·ⲈⲒ Ⲁ·ⲚⲞⲨⲬⲈ Ⲛ̄·ϨⲚ̄·
they-know not that I-have-come to-cast some-

·ⲠⲰⲢⲬˋ ⲈⲬⲚ̄·Ⲡ·ⲔⲀϨ ⲞⲨ·ⲔⲰϨⲦ ⲞⲨ·ⲤⲎϤⲈˋ
-divisions upon-the-earth - (a)fire, (a)sword,

ⲞⲨ·ⲠⲞⲖⲈⲘⲞⲤ ⲞⲨⲚ̄·ⲦⲞⲨ ⲄⲀⲢ ·ⲚⲀ·ϢⲰ[ⲠⲈ]
(a)war, > (for) (there-are)five, (---), will-come-to-be

ϨⲚ̄·ⲞⲨ·ⲎⲒ ⲞⲨⲚ̄·ϢⲞⲘⲦ ·ⲚⲀ·ϢⲰⲠⲈ ⲈⲬⲚ̄·
in-a-house; (there-are)three will-come-to-be against-

·ⲤⲚⲀⲨ ⲀⲨⲰ ⲤⲚⲀⲨ ⲈⲬⲚ̄·ϢⲞⲘⲦˋ Ⲡ·ⲈⲒⲰⲦˋ
-two, and two against-three; the-father

ⲈⲬⲘ̄·Ⲡ·ϢⲎⲢⲈ ⲀⲨⲰ Ⲡ·ϢⲎⲢⲈ ⲈⲬⲘ̄·Ⲡ·ⲈⲒⲰⲦˋ
against-the-son, and the-son against-the-father;

ⲀⲨⲰˋ ⲤⲈ·ⲚⲀ·ⲰϨⲈ Ⲉ·ⲢⲀⲦ·ⲞⲨ ⲈⲨ·Ⲟ Ⲙ̄·ⲘⲞⲚⲀ-
and they-will-stand to-their-feet, they-being single-

-ⲬⲞⲤ ⲠⲈⲬⲈ·ⲒⲤ ⲬⲈ Ⲧ·ⲚⲀ·Ⲧ ⲚⲎ·ⲦⲚ̄ Ⲙ̄·ⲠⲈⲦⲈ·
-ones.

Jesus said, "Men think, perhaps, that it is peace which I have come to cast upon the world. They do not know that it is dissension which I have come to cast upon the earth: fire, sword, and war. For there will be five in a house: three will be against two, and two against three, the father against the son, and the son against the father. And they will stand solitary."

INTERPRETATION:

The verse is analogous to

Matthew 10:34-36

"Do not think that I came to bring peace

on earth. I did not come to bring peace but a sword. For I have come to 'set a man against his father, a daughter against her mother, and a daughter-in-law against her mother-in-law; and a man's enemies will be those of his household.' "

17

ΠΕΧΕ·ΙC	ΧΕ	†·ΝΑ·†	ΝΗ·ΤΝ	Μ·ΠΕΤΕ·
Said Jesus	this:	I-will-give	to-you(pl)	that-which-

ΠΕ·ΒΑΛ	·ΝΑΥ	ΕΡΟ·Ϥ	ΑΥΩ	ΠΕΤΕ·ΜΠΕ·ΜΑ-
-did-not-eye	look	upon-him,	and	he-who-did-not-e-

-ΑΧΕ	·CΟΤΜ·ΕϤ	ΑΥΩ	ΠΕΤΕ·ΜΠΕ·ϬΙΧ	·ϬΜ-
-ar	hear-him,	and	he-who-did-not-hand	tou-

-ϬΩΜ·Ϥ	ΑΥΩ	ΜΠΕϤ·\·ΕΙ	Ε·2ΡΑΪ	2Ι·ΦΗΤ
-ch-him,	and	did-not-he\come	up	on-the-mind

Ρ·ΡΩΜΕ
of-man.

Jesus said, "I shall give you what no eye has seen and what no ear has heard and what no hand has touched and what has never occurred to the human mind."

INTERPRETATION:

The verse is analogous to

1 Corinthians 2:9

"But as it is written: 'Eye has not seen, nor ear heard, nor have entered into the heart of man the things which God has prepared for those who love Him.'"

18

ΠΕΧΕ·Μ·ΜΑΘΗΤΗC		Ν·ΙC	ΧΕ	·ΧΟ·
Said-the-disciples		to-	this:	Spe-

·ΟC	ΕΡΟ·Ν	ΧΕ	ΤΝ·2ΑΗ	ΕC·ΝΑ·ϢΩΠΕ	Ν·
-ak	to-us	this-	our-end,	she-will-come-to-be	in-

·ΑϢ	Ν·2Ε	ΠΕΧΕ·ΙC	<>	ΑΤΕΤΝ·6ΩΛΠ'	ΓΑΡ	ΕΒΟΛ
-which	way?	*Said-JS20	(this)	Have-you(pl)-revealed,	(--),	forth

Ν·Τ·ΑΡΧΗ	ΧΕΚΛΑC	ΕΤΕΤΝΑ·ϢΙΝΕ	ΝCΑ·
the-beginning,	sothat	you(pl)-will-be-seeking	after-

·ΘΑ2Η	ΧΕ	2Μ·Π·ΜΑ	ΕΤΕ	Τ·ΑΡΧΗ	Μ·ΜΑΥ	Ε·
-the-end?	for	in-the-place	which	the-beginning (is)	there,	-

·ΘΑ2Η	·ΝΑ·ϢΩΠΕ	Μ·ΜΑΥ	ΟΥ·ΜΑΚΑΡΙΟC
-the-end	will-come-to-be	there;	> a-blessed-one,

ΠΕΤ·ΝΑ·Ω2Ε	Ε·ΡΑΤ·ϥ	2Ν·Τ·ΑΡΧΗ	ΑΥΩ
he-who-will-stand	to-his-feet	in-the-beginning,	and

ϥ·ΝΑ·CΟΥΩΝ·Θ2ΑΗ	ΑΥΩ	ϥ·ΝΑ·ΧΙ·†ΠΕ
he-will-know-the-end,	and	he-will-take-taste

ΑΝ	Μ·ΜΟΥ
not	of-death.

The disciples said to Jesus. "Tell us how our end will be." Jesus said, "Have you discovered, then, the beginning, thatyou look for the end? For where the beginning is, there will be the end. Blessed is he who will take his place in the beginning; he will know the end and will not experience death."

INTERPRETATION:

Jesus is the Alpha and the Omega, the beginning, and the end of all created things.

From Him, we proceed, and to Him we return by believing in Him.

As far as eternity is concerned, the earth cannot define the beginning nor the end of all created things because nothing originated in the material world, nor can it determine the fate of things.

19

ⲡⲉⲝⲉ·ⲓⲥ ⲭⲉ ⲟⲩ·ⲙⲁⲕⲁⲣⲓⲟⲥ
Said Jesus this: A-blessed-one

ⲡⲉ ⲛⲧⲁϩ·ϣⲱⲡⲉ ϩⲁ·ⲧ·ⲉϩⲏ ⲉⲙⲡⲁⲧⲉϥ·ϣⲱ-
is-he who-came-into-being from-the-beginning, before-he-came-to-

-ⲡⲉ ⲉⲧⲉⲧⲛ·ϣⲁⲛ·ϣⲱⲡⲉ ⲛⲁ·ⲉⲓ ⲙ·ⲙⲁⲑⲏ-
-be. > If-you(pl)-should-come-to-be to-me disci-

-ⲧⲏⲥ ⲛⲧⲉⲧⲛ·ⲥⲱⲧⲙ ⲁ·ⲛⲁ·ϣⲁⲝⲉ ⲛⲉⲉⲓ·ⲱ-
-ples, &-you(pl)-listen to-my-words, these-sto-

-ⲛⲉ ·ⲛⲁ·ⲣ·ⲇⲓⲁⲕⲟⲛⲉⲓ ⲛⲏ·ⲧⲛ ⲟⲩⲛ·ⲧⲏ·ⲧⲛ
-nes will-become-servants to-you(pl), > (for) have-you(pl),

ⲅⲁⲣ· ⲙ·ⲙⲁⲩ ⲛ·ϯⲟⲩ ⲛ·ϣⲏⲛ ϩⲙ·ⲡⲁⲣⲁ·\
(---), there five trees in-para-\

-ⲇⲓⲥⲟⲥ ⲉ·ⲥⲉ·ⲕⲓⲙ ⲁⲛ ⲛ·ϣⲱⲙ· ⲙ·ⲡⲣⲱ
-dise which()move not summer (and?) winter,

ⲁⲩⲱ ⲙⲁⲣⲉ·ⲛⲟⲩ·ϭⲱⲃⲉ ·ϩⲉ ⲉⲃⲟⲗ ⲡⲉⲧ·\
and do-not-their-leaves fall down. > He-who-\

·ⲛⲁ·ⲥⲟⲩⲱⲛ·ⲟⲩ ϥ·ⲛⲁ·ϫⲓ·ϯⲡⲉ ⲁⲛ· ⲙ·ⲙⲟⲩ
-will-know-them, he-will-take-taste not of-death.

Jesus said, "Blessed is he who came into being before he came into being. If you become my disciples and listen to my words, these stones will minister to you. For there are five trees for you in Paradise which remain undisturbed summer and winter and whose leaves do not fall. Whoever becomes acquainted with them will not experience death."

INTERPRETATION:

The first part of the verse is analogous to the blessing we have received since our pre-existence in God, as Paul mentions in the Epistle to the **Ephesians 1:3-4**.

"Blessed be the God and Father of our Lord Jesus Christ, who has blessed us with every spiritual blessing in the heavenly places in Christ, just as He chose us in Him before the foundation of the world, that we should be holy and blameless before Him in love."

The trees refer to Christ himself, the tree of life, who is the giver of eternal life. In the book of Revelation, the tree appears on both sides of the river in multiple ways.

 Revelation 22:2

"In the middle of its street, and on either side of the river, was the tree of life, which bore twelve fruits, each tree yielding its fruit every month. The leaves of the tree were for the healing of the nations."

In this plurality, we can see the number five as the number that symbolizes the nature of Christ, who extends his grace and manifestation through five ministries.

The trees Jesus mentions do not change their leaves. It speaks of the immutability and faithfulness of God to man. Knowing Him leads us to eternal life.

We can also see the number five in the Tabernacle of Moses in the wilderness representing God dwelling among his people in a tent of skins. Everything in the Tabernacle foreshadowed Christ coming in the flesh.

It had five pillars at the entrance to the Holy Place, representing Christ Himself, the only access to the Kingdom of God and Paradise.

To the Church of Philadelphia in Revelation, God grants them to be these pillars. (Revelation 22:2)

> "He who overcomes, I will make him a pillar in the temple of My God, and he shall go out no more. I will write on him the name of My God and the name of the city of My God, the New Jerusalem, which comes down out of heaven from My God. And I will write on him My new name."

In the apocryphal gospel of Philip, there are paragraphs inconsistent with the Bible (which we do not approve of), but others are extraordinary. One of them is verse 68, which sheds light on this difficult passage of Thomas.

> " The Lord did everything in a mystery: a baptism, an anointing, a Communion (Lord's Supper,) a redemption (by the

cross and Christ's sacrifice,) and a bridal chamber (the union of the Spirit of God with the spirit of man 1 Corinthians 6:17)" **(Gospel of Phillip 68).**

These five elements of Christ's work in the believer are five columns or trees that one must eat spiritually. In other words, we must meditate on them until they become flesh in us as proper nourishment.

20

ΠΕΧΕ·Μ·ΜΑΘΗΤΗΣ ΧΕ ·ΧΟ·ΟΣ
Said-the-disciples this: Speak

ΕΡΟ·Ν ΧΕ Τ·ΜΝΤΕΡΟ·Ν·Μ·ΠΗΥΕ ΕΣ·
to-us this- the-kingdom-of(the)heaven(s), she-

·ΤΝΤⲰΝ Ε·ΝΙΜ ΠΕΧΑ·ϥ ΝΑ·Υ ΧΕ ΕⲤ·ΤΝ-
-compares to-whom? > Said-he to-them this: she-com-

-ΤⲰΝ Α·Υ·ΒΑΒΙΛΕ Ν·ϢΛΤΑΜ ⲤΟⲂΚ ΠΑ-
-pares to-a-grain of-mustard > small, more-

-ΡΑ·Ν·ϬΡΟϬ ΤΗΡ·ΟΥ ϨΟΤΑΝ ΔΕ ΕⲤ·ϢΑ ·
-than-the-seeds, allofthem; > when, hwvr, she-should-

·ϨΕ ΕΧⲘ·Π·ΚΑϨ ΕΤ·ΟΥ·Ⲣ·ϨⲰⲂ ΕΡΟ·ϥ ϢΑϥ·
-fall onto-the-earth which-they-did-work on-him, does-he-

·ΤΕΥΟ ΕⲂΟΛ Ν·ΝΟΥ·ΝΟϬ Ν·ΤΑΡ Νϥ·ϢⲰ-
-send out a-great branch &()-comes-to-

-ΠΕ Ν·ⲤΚΕΠΗ Ν·ϨΑΛΑΤΕ Ν·Τ·ΠΕ
-be shelter (for) the-birds of-the-sky.

The disciples said to Jesus, "Tell us what the kingdom of heaven is like." He said to them, "It is

like a mustard seed. It is the smallest of all seeds. But when it falls on tilled soil, it produces a great plant and becomes a shelter for birds of the sky."

INTERPRETATION:

This saying is parallel to

 Matthew 13:31-32

"A good man out of the good treasure of his heart brings forth good; and an evil man out of the evil treasure of his heart brings forth evil. For out of the abundance of the heart his mouth speaks."

ⲡⲉ-
> Sa-

-ⲭⲉ·ⲙⲁⲣⲓϩⲁⲙ   Ⲛ·ⲓⲥ   ⲭⲉ   ⲉ·ⲛⲉⲕ·ⲙⲁⲑⲏ-
-id-Mariam   to-Jesus   this: Do-your(sg)-disci-

-ⲧⲏⲥ ·ⲉⲓⲛⲉ   Ⲛ·ⲛⲓⲙ`   ⲡⲉⲭⲁ·ϥ`   ⲭⲉ   ⲉⲩ·ⲉⲓⲛⲉ
-ples resemble   whom?   > Said-he   this: They-resemble

Ⲛ·ϩⲛ·ϣⲏⲣⲉ·ϣⲏⲙ`   ⲉⲩ·[ϭ]ⲉⲗⲓⲧ`   ⲁ·ⲩ·ⲥⲱϣⲉ   ⲉ·ⲧⲱ·
()-small-children   ()dwelling   in-a-field   which-th-

·ⲟⲩ ⲁⲛ ⲧⲉ   ϩⲟⲧⲁⲛ   ⲉⲩ·ϣⲁ·ⲉⲓ   Ⲛϭⲓ·Ⲛ·ⲭⲟⲉⲓⲥ
-eirs   not   is.   > When   they-should-come,   viz-the-Lords

Ⲛ·ⲧ·ⲥⲱϣⲉ   ⲥⲉ·ⲛⲁ·ⲭⲟ·ⲟⲥ   ⲭⲉ   ·ⲕⲉ·ⲧⲛ·ⲥⲱϣⲉ
of-the-field,   they-will-speak   this-   "Give-our-field

ⲉⲃⲟⲗ ⲛⲁ·ⲛ   Ⲛ·ⲧⲟ·ⲟⲩ   ⲥⲉ·ⲕⲁⲕ   ⲁ·ϩⲏⲩ   Ⲙ·ⲡⲟⲩ·Ⲙ-
back   to-us."   > They,   ()-strip   naked   in-their-pres-

-ⲧⲟ ⲉⲃⲟⲗ ⲉⲧⲣⲟⲩ·ⲕⲁⲁ·ⲥ   ⲉⲃⲟⲗ ⲛⲁ·ⲩ   Ⲛⲥⲉ·ϯ·ⲧⲟⲩ·
-ence   ( )   that-they-give-her   back   to-them   &-they-give-their-

·ⲥⲱϣⲉ ⲛⲁ·ⲩ   ⲇⲓⲁ·ⲧⲟⲩⲧⲟ   ϯ·ⲭⲱ   Ⲙ·ⲙⲟ·ⲥ   ⲭⲉ   ⲉϥ·`
-field   to-them.   > Therefore,   I-speak   of-it   thus: If-he\

·ϣⲁ·ⲉⲓⲙⲉ   Ⲛϭⲓ·ⲡ·ⲭⲉⲥ·ϩⲛ·ϩⲉⲓ   ⲭⲉ   ϥ·ⲛⲏⲩ   Ⲛϭⲓ·
-should-realize,   viz-the-Lord-of-the-house,   that   he-is-coming,   viz-

·ⲡ·ⲣⲉϥ·ⲭⲓⲟⲩⲉ   ϥ·ⲛⲁ·ⲣⲟⲉⲓⲥ   ⲉⲙⲡⲁⲧⲉϥ·`·ⲉⲓ   Ⲛϥ·ⲧⲙ·
-the-robber,   he-will-keep-watch   before-he-\-come   &-()-not-

·ⲕⲁⲁ·ϥ`   ⲉ·ϣⲟⲭⲧ`   ⲉϩⲟⲩⲛ   ⲉ·ⲡⲉϥ·ⲏⲉⲓ   Ⲛⲧⲉ·ⲧⲉϥ·`
-permit-him   to-tunnel   in   to-his-house   of-his\

·ⲙⲚⲧⲉⲣⲟ   ⲉⲧⲣⲉϥ·ϥⲓ   Ⲛ·ⲛⲉϥ·`·ⲥⲕⲉⲩⲟⲥ   Ⲛ·ⲧⲱ·ⲧⲛ
-kingdom   that-he-take   his-   \ -goods.   > You(pl),

ⲇⲉ   ·ⲣⲟⲉⲓⲥ   ϩⲁ·ⲧ·ⲉϩⲏ   Ⲙ·ⲡ·ⲕⲟⲥⲙⲟⲥ   ·ⲙⲟⲩⲣ`   Ⲙ·
hwvr,   keep-watch   from-the-beginning   of-the-world;   > bind   -

·ⲙⲱ·ⲧⲛ   ⲉⲭⲛ·ⲛⲉⲧⲛ·ϯⲡⲉ   ϩⲛ·ⲛⲟⲩ·ⲛⲟϭ   Ⲛ·ⲇⲩ-
-you(pl)   onto-your(pl)-loins   in-a-great   pow-

-ⲛⲁⲙⲓⲥ ϣⲓⲛⲁ   ⲭⲉ   ⲛⲉ·ⲛ·ⲗⲏⲥⲧⲏⲥ   ·ϩⲉ   ⲉ·ϩⲓⲏ   ⲉ·ⲉⲓ
-er,   so   that   not-the-thieves   fall   on(a)road   to-come

ϣⲁⲣⲱ·ⲧⲛ   ⲉⲡⲉⲓ   ⲧⲉ·ⲭⲣⲉⲓⲁ   ⲉⲧⲉⲧⲛ·ϭⲱϣⲧ`
upto-you(pl),   because   the-help   which-you(pl)-look

ⲉⲃⲟⲗ   ϩⲏⲧ·ⲥ   ⲥⲉ·ⲛⲁ·ϩⲉ   ⲉⲣⲟ·ⲥ   ⲙⲁⲣⲉϥ·ϣⲱⲡⲉ
outward   for-her,   they-will-fall   upon-her.   > Let-him-come-to-be

ϩⲛ·ⲧⲉⲧⲛ·ⲙⲏⲧⲉ   Ⲛϭⲓ·ⲟⲩ·ⲣⲱⲙⲉ   Ⲛ·ⲉⲡⲓⲥⲧⲏ-
in-your(pl)-midst,   viz-a-man   (of)understand-

-ⲙⲱⲛ   Ⲛⲧⲁⲣⲉ·ⲡ·ⲕⲁⲣⲡⲟⲥ   ·ⲡⲱϩ   ⲁϥ·ⲉⲓ   ϩⲛ·ⲛⲟⲩ·
-ing.   > When-the-fruit   split(open),   he-came   in-a-

·ϭⲉⲡⲏ   ⲉ·ⲡⲉϥ·ⲁⲥϩ   ϩⲛ·ⲧⲉϥ·ϭⲓⲭ   ⲁϥ·ϩⲁⲥ·ϥ   ⲡⲉ-
-hurry,   his-sickle   in-his-hand;   he-reaped-him.   > He-

-ⲧⲉ·ⲟⲩⲛ·ⲙⲁⲁⲭⲉ   Ⲙ·ⲙⲟ·ϥ`   ⲉ·ⲥⲱⲧⲙ   ⲙⲁⲣⲉϥ·ⲥⲱⲧⲙ
-who-has-ear   of-him   to-listen,   let-him-listen.

Mary said to Jesus, "Who are your disciples like?"
He said, "They are like children who have settled
in a field which is not theirs. When the owners of
the field come, they will say, 'Let us have back our
field.' They (will) undress in their presence to let
them have back their field and give it back to them.
Therefore, I say if the owner of a house knows that
the thief is coming, he will begin his vigil before
he comes and will not let him dig through into the
house of his domain to carry away his goods. You
(pl.), then, be on your guard against the world. Arm
yourselves with great strength lest the robbers
find a way to come to you, for the difficulty which
you expect will (surely) materialize. Let there be
among you a man of understanding. When the
grain ripened, he came quickly with his sickle in
his hand and reaped it. Whoever has ears to hear,
let him hear."

INTERPRETATION:

Matthew 24:43

The first part of this verse is similar to the parable of the vineyard in which the laborers work for a vineyard that is not theirs. Subsequently, Jesus refers to what is stated in the Gospel of Matthew: "But know this, that if the father of the house knew at what hour the thief would come, he would watch and not let his house be broken into.

Second, this gospel uses the term system repeatedly. It helps to understand the term 'world,' which appears in other canon books. System and World are collective and individual beliefs that form the consciousness of our society. They are the source of the guiding mindset of nations, cultures, and particular viewpoints.

He quotes from the book of Job 3:25, "For the thing I greatly feared has come upon me, and that which I dreaded has happened to me."

Jesus issues a warning against this world's system as the tool the enemy uses to steal and destroy. He ends by speaking of the Kingdom of God, where he protects and guards what is his.

22

ⲡⲉϫⲁ·ϥ ⲛ̄·
Said-he to-
·ⲛⲉϥ·ⲙⲁⲑⲏⲧⲏⲥ ϫⲉ ⲛⲉⲉⲓ·ⲕⲟⲩⲉⲓ ⲉⲧ·ϫⲓ·ⲉⲣⲱ-
-his-disciples this: These-little-ones who-take-mil-
-ⲧⲉ ⲉⲩ·ⲧⲛ̄ⲧⲱⲛ ⲁ·ⲛⲉⲧ·ⲃⲏⲕ` ⲉϩⲟⲩⲛ ⲁ·ⲧ·ⲙⲛ̄-
-k, they-compare to-those-who-go in to-the-king-
-ⲧⲉⲣⲟ ⲡⲉϫⲁ·ⲩ ⲛⲁ·ϥ` ϫⲉ ⲉⲉⲓⲉ ⲛ·ⲟ ⲛ̄·ⲕⲟⲩⲉⲓ ⲧⲛ̄·
-dom. > Said-they to-him this: then, ()being little-ones, we-
·ⲛⲁ·ⲃⲱⲕ` ⲉϩⲟⲩⲛ ⲉ·ⲧ·ⲙⲛ̄ⲧⲉⲣⲟ ⲡⲉϫⲉ·ⲓⲏⲥ ⲛⲁ·ⲩ
-will-go in to-the-kingdom? > Said-*JES2* to-them
ϫⲉ ϩⲟⲧⲁⲛ ⲉⲧⲉⲧⲛ̄·ϣⲁ·ⲣ̄·ⲡ·ⲥⲛⲁⲩ ⲟⲩⲁ ⲁⲩⲱ ⲉ-
this: when you(pl)-should-make-the-two one, and if-
-ⲧⲉⲧⲛ̄·ϣⲁ·ⲣ̄·ⲡ·ⲥⲁ·ⲛ·ϩⲟⲩⲛ ⲛ̄·ⲑⲉ ⲙ̄·ⲡ·ⲥⲁ·ⲛ·ⲃⲟⲗ
-you(pl)-should-make-the-side-inner like the-side-outer,
ⲁⲩⲱ ⲡ·ⲥⲁ·ⲛ·ⲃⲟⲗ ⲛ̄·ⲑⲉ ⲙ̄·ⲡ·ⲥⲁ·ⲛ·ϩⲟⲩⲛ ..(ⲱ ⲡ·ⲥⲁ·
and the-side-outer like the-side-inner, and the-side-
·ⲧ·ⲡⲉ ⲛ̄·ⲑⲉ ⲙ̄·ⲡ·ⲥⲁ·ⲙ·ⲡ·ⲓⲧⲛ̄ ⲁⲩⲱ ϣⲓⲛⲁ ⲉⲧⲉ-
-upper like the-side-lower, > and so you-
-ⲧⲛⲁ·ⲉⲓⲣⲉ ⲙ̄·ⲫⲟ`ⲟⲩⲧ` ⲙⲛ̄·ⲧ·ⲥϩⲓⲙⲉ ⲙ̄·ⲡⲓ·ⲟⲩⲁ
-(pl)-will-be-making the-ma\ le and-the-woman that-one
ⲟⲩⲱⲧ` ϫⲉⲕⲁⲁⲥ ⲛⲉ·ⲫⲟⲟⲩⲧ` ·ⲣ̄·ϩⲟⲟⲩⲧ` ⲛ̄ⲧⲉ·
alone, sothat not-the-male become-male, (nor)-
·ⲧ·ⲥϩⲓⲙⲉ ·ⲣ̄·ⲥϩⲓⲙⲉ ϩⲟⲧⲁⲛ ⲉⲧⲉⲧⲛ̄·ϣⲁ·ⲉⲓⲣⲉ
-the-woman become-woman; > when you(pl)-should-make
ⲛ̄·ϩⲛ̄·ⲃⲁⲗ ⲉ·ⲡ·ⲙⲁ ⲛ̄·ⲟⲩ·ⲃⲁⲗ` ⲁⲩⲱ ⲟⲩ·ϭⲓϫ`
some-eyes to-the-place of-an-eye, and a-hand
ⲉ·ⲡ·ⲙⲁ ⲛ̄·ⲛⲟⲩ·ϭⲓϫ` ⲁⲩⲱ ⲟⲩ·ⲉⲣⲏⲧⲉ ⲉ·ⲡ·ⲙⲁ
to-the-place of-a-hand, and a-foot to-the-place
ⲛ̄·ⲟⲩ·ⲉⲣⲏⲧⲉ ⲟⲩ·ϩⲓⲕⲱⲛ` ⲉ·ⲡ·ⲙⲁ ⲛ̄·ⲟⲩ·ϩⲓⲕⲱ̄
of-a-foot; an-image to-the-place of-an-image,
ⲧⲟⲧⲉ ⲧⲉⲧⲛⲁ·ⲃⲱⲕ` ⲉϩⲟⲩⲛ [ⲉ·ⲧ·ⲙⲛ̄ⲧⲉⲣⲟ]
then you(pl)-will-go in to-the-kingdom.

Jesus saw infants being suckled. He said to his disciples, "These infants being suckled are like those who enter the kingdom." They said to him, "Shall we then, as children, enter the kingdom?" Jesus said to them, "When you make the two one, and when you make the inside like the outside and the outside like the inside, and the above like the below, and when you make the male and the female one and the same, so that the male not be male nor the female; and when you fashion eyes in place of an eye, and a hand in place of a hand, and a foot in place of a foot, and a likeness in place of a likeness; then will you enter [the kingdom]."

INTERPRETATION:

The first part is parallel to

Matthew 18:3
"and said, 'Assuredly, I say to you, unless you are converted and become as little children, you will by no means enter the kingdom of heaven.'"

"That they all may be one..." Jesus taught about the oneness between Him and the Father. "The Father and I are one", and He prayed that we might also be one. "That they all may be one, as You, Father, are in Me, and I in You; that they also may be one in Us, that the world may believe that You sent Me." (John 17:21)

"And make the inside as the outside and the outside as the inside" This speaks of the wholeness and integrity of a true Christian. What is within us, Christ Himself must be seen visibly through our works and our love for our neighbor.

"And the above like the below." Jesus said to the Pharisees: "You are from beneath; I am from above." What is in heaven must be reflected on the earth so the world may recognize the redemption of Christ. (John 8:23)

"And when you make the male and the female one and the same so that the male is not male nor the female." It speaks to us of returning things to the way they were at the beginning when there was no male and female but one being -Adam- in whom the feminine and masculine were united. It refers to the likeness of God that comes from the Spirit, where there is no longer Jew and Greek, male and female, but one united body, which is the body of Jesus.

The last part, where we see the exchange of eyes, feet, and image, speaks to us of exchanging our human perception for that of God, our works and walk for His, and our distorted image for His image.

23

ΠΕΧΕ·ΙC	ΧΕ	†·ΝΑ·CΕ[Τ]Π·ΤΗΝΕ	ΟΥΑ	ΕΒΟΛ
Said Jesus	this:	I-will-choose-you(pl),	one	out
2Ν·ϢΟ	ΑΥω	CΝΑΥ	ΕΒΟΛ	2Ν·ΤΒΑ	ΑΥω
of-1000,	and	two	out	of-10000,	> and
CΕ·ΝΑ·ω2Ε	Ε·ΡΑΤ·ΟΥ	ΕΥ·Ο	ΟΥΑ	ΟΥωΤ`	ΠΕ-
they-will-stand	to-their-feet,	they-being	one	alone.	

Jesus said, "I shall choose you, one out of a thousand, and two out of ten thousand, and they shall stand as a single one."

INTERPRETATION:

This saying is analogous to

Matthew 22:14
"For many are called, but few are chosen."

These chosen ones are those who, dying to themselves, seek the oneness of the Father to reflect heaven on earth. They do not seek to exalt their names but only that Jesus and his love may be seen.

24

Sa-

-ⲭⲉ·ⲚⲈϤ·ⲘⲀⲐⲎⲦⲎⲤ   ⲬⲈ   ⲘⲀ·ⲦⲤⲈⲂⲞ·Ⲛˋ   Ⲉ·ⲡ·ⲦⲞ-
-id-his-disciples   this: Show-us   to-the-pl-

-ⲠⲞⲤ   ⲈⲦ·Ⲕ·Ⲙ̄·ⲘⲀⲨ   ⲈⲠⲈⲒ   ⲦⲀⲚⲀⲄⲔⲎ   ⲈⲢⲞ·Ⲛ   ⲦⲈ
-ace   which-you(sg)(are)there,   because   necessary   to-us (it) is

ⲈⲦⲠ̄Ⲛ̄·ϢⲒⲚⲈ   Ⲛ̄Ⲥⲱ·Ϥˋ   ⲠⲈⲬⲀ·Ϥˋ   ⲚⲀ·Ⲩ   ⲬⲈ   ⲠⲈⲦ·ⲈⲨ-
that-we-seek   after-him. > Said-he   to-them   this: he-who-ha-

-Ⲛ̄·ⲘⲀⲀⲬⲈ   Ⲙ̄·ⲘⲞ·Ϥ   ⲘⲀⲢⲈϤ·ˋ·ⲤⲱⲦⲘ̄   ⲞⲨⲚ̄·ⲞⲨ-
-s-ear   of-him,   let-him- \ -listen;   > There-is-l-

-ⲞⲈⲒⲚˋ   ·ϢⲞⲞⲠˋ   Ⲙ̄·ⲪⲞⲨⲚ   Ⲛ̄·ⲚⲞⲨ·Ⲣ̄Ⲙ·ⲞⲨⲞⲈⲒⲚ
-ight   exists   in-the-inner   of-a-man-of-light

ⲀⲨⲱ   Ϥ·Ⲣ̄·ⲞⲨⲞⲈⲒⲚ   Ⲉ·Π·ⲔⲞⲤⲘⲞⲤ   ⲦⲎⲢ·Ϥˋ   ⲈϤ·ⲦⲘ̄·
and   he-becomes-light   to-the-world,   all-of-it;   if-he-not-

·Ⲣ̄·ⲞⲨⲞⲈⲒⲚˋ   ⲞⲨ·ⲔⲀⲔⲈ   ⲠⲈ   ⲠⲈⲬⲈ·Ⲓ̄Ⲥ̄   ⲬⲈ   ·ⲘⲈⲢⲈ·
-become-light,   (a)darkness   is-he.

His disciples said to him, "Show us the place where you are since it is necessary for us to seek it." He said to them, "Whoever has ears, let him hear. There is light within a man of light, and he lights up the whole world. If he does not shine, he is darkness."

INTERPRETATION:

God is Light, and as our spirit comes into unity with Him, His Light radiates from within us. The natural mind opposes the Spirit and blocks it like a bronze shell that keeps the Light from being perceived.

That is why when we walk and operate from our carnal mind, we find ourselves in darkness, unable to produce any change in our environment.

In the gospel of Matthew, Jesus spoke to his disciples about the Light that dwelt in them. This was said long before they had received the Holy Spirit. It is the Light of the Father's life placed in the sons of God from before the foundation of the world, which begins to shine when connected to Jesus.

Matthew 5:14-16
"You are the light of the world. A city that is set on a hill cannot be hidden. Nor do they light a lamp and put it under a basket, but on a lampstand, and

it gives light to all who are in the house. Let your light so shine before men, that they may see your good works and glorify your Father in heaven."

25

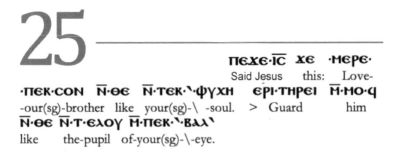

ΠΕΧΕ·ΙС ΧΕ ·ΜΕΡΕ·
Said Jesus this: Love-

·ΠΕΚ·СΟΝ Ν·ΘΕ Ν·ΤΕΚ·ʾ·ΨΥΧΗ ΕΡΙ·ΤΗΡΕΙ Μ·ΜΟ·Ϥ
-our(sg)-brother like your(sg)-\ -soul. > Guard him

Ν·ΘΕ Ν·Τ·ΕΛΟΥ Μ·ΠΕΚ·ʾ·ΒΑΛʾ
like the-pupil of-your(sg)-\-eye.

Jesus said, "Love your brother like your soul; guard him like the pupil of your eye."

INTERPRETATION:

This saying is analogous with

 Matthew 22:39

"And the second is like it: 'You shall love your neighbor as yourself.' "

26

ⲡⲉⲝⲉ·ⲓ̅ⲥ̅ ⲝⲉ ⲡ·ⲭⲏ
Said Jesus this: the-mote

ⲉⲧ·ⲅ̅ⲙ̅·ⲡ·ⲃⲁⲗ ⲙ̅·ⲡⲉⲕ·`·ⲥⲟⲛ ⲕ·ⲛⲁⲩ ⲉⲡⲟ·ϥ` ⲡ·ⲥⲟⲉⲓ
()in-the-eye of-your(sg)-\-brother, you(sg)-see him; the-beam,

ⲁⲉ ⲉⲧ·ⲅ̅ⲙ̅·ⲡⲉⲕ·ⲃⲁⲗ` ⲕ·ⲛⲁⲩ ⲁⲛ ⲉⲡⲟ·ϥ` ⲅⲟⲧⲁⲛ
hwvr, ()-in-your(sg)-eye, you(sg)-see not it/him; > when

ⲉⲕ·ⲱⲁⲛ·ⲛⲟⲩⲝⲉ ⲙ̅·ⲡ·ⲥⲟⲉⲓ ⲉⲃⲟⲗ ⲅ̅ⲙ̅·ⲡⲉⲕ·`
you(sg)-should-cast the-beam out of-your(sg)\

·ⲃⲁⲗ` ⲧⲟⲧⲉ ⲕ·ⲛⲁ·ⲛⲁⲩ ⲉⲃⲟⲗ ⲉ·ⲛⲟⲩⲝⲉ ⲙ̅·ⲡ·ⲭⲏ
-eye, then you(sg)-will-see outward to-cast the-mote

ⲉⲃⲟⲗ ⲅ̅ⲙ̅·ⲡ·ⲃⲁⲗ ⲙ̅·ⲡⲉⲕ·ⲥⲟⲛ
out of-the-eye of-your(sg)-brother.

Jesus said, "You see the mote in your brother's eye, but you do not see the beam in your own eye. When you cast the beam out of your own eye, then you will see clearly to cast the mote from your brother's eye."

INTERPRETATION:

This verse is analogous to

Matthew 7:3-5

"And why do you look at the speck in your brother's eye but do not consider the plank in your own eye? Or how can you say to your brother, 'Let me remove the speck from your eye'; and look, a plank is in your own eye? Hypocrite! First remove the plank from your own eye, and then you will see clearly to remove the speck from your brother's eye."

27

ⲈⲦⲈⲦⲘ·Ⲡ·ⲚⲎ-
If-you(pl)-do-not-fa-

-ⲤⲦⲈⲨⲈ Ⲉ·Ⲡ·ⲔⲞⲤⲘⲞⲤ ⲦⲈⲦⲚⲀ·ϨⲈ ⲀⲚˋ Ⲉ·Ⲧ·ⲘⲚ̄ⲦⲈ-
-st   to-the-world,   you(pl)-will-fall   not   to-the-king-

-ⲢⲞ   ⲈⲦⲈⲦⲚ̄·ⲦⲘ̄·ⲈⲒⲢⲈ   Ⲙ̄·Ⲡ·ⲤⲀⲘⲂⲀⲦⲞⲚ   Ⲛ̄·ⲤⲀⲂˋ
-dom; >   if-you(pl)-do-not-make   the-sabbath(sp)   sab\

-ⲂⲀⲦⲞⲚ   Ⲛ̄ⲦⲈⲦⲚⲀ·ⲚⲀⲨ   ⲀⲚ   Ⲉ·Ⲡ·ⲈⲒⲰⲦˋ
-bath,   you(pl)-will-look   not   upon-the-father.

Jesus said, "If you do not fast the world (system), you will not find the kingdom. If you do not make the Sabbath the (true) Sabbath, you will not see the father."

INTERPRETATION:

Clement of Alexandria in Stromateis 3.15.99.4 added a beatitude with similar content:

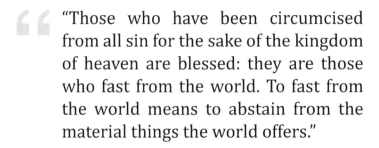

> "Those who have been circumcised from all sin for the sake of the kingdom of heaven are blessed: they are those who fast from the world. To fast from the world means to abstain from the material things the world offers."

In a broader sense, it implies fasting from the dependencies on the system that binds us, to break their power over us.

28

ΠΕΧΕ·ⲓ̅ⲥ̅
Said Jesus

ⲭⲉ   ⲁⲉⲓ·ⲱ2ⲉ   ⲉ·ⲣⲁⲧ·ˋ   2ⲛ̅·ⲧ·ⲙⲏⲧⲉ   ⲙ̅·ⲡ·ⲕⲟⲥ-
this: Did-I-stand   to-my-feet   in-the-midst   of-the-wo-

-ⲙⲟⲥ   ⲁⲩⲱ   ⲁⲉⲓ·ⲟⲩⲱⲛ2   ⲉⲃⲟⲗ   ⲛⲁ·ⲩ   2ⲛ̅·ⲥⲁⲣ2̄
-rld,   and   did-I-appear   outwardly   to-them   in-flesh;

ⲁⲉⲓ·2ⲉ   ⲉⲣⲟ·ⲟⲩ   ⲧⲏⲣ·ⲟⲩ   ⲉⲩ·ⲧⲁ2ⲉ   ⲙ̄ⲡⲓ·2ⲉ   ⲉ·ⲗⲁ-
Did-I-fall   upon-them,   all-of-them,   ()drunk;   did-not-I-fall   on-any-

-ⲁⲩ   ⲛ̅·2ⲏⲧ·ⲟⲩ   ⲉϥ·ⲟⲃⲉ   ⲁⲩⲱ   ⲁ·ⲧⲁ·ⲯⲩⲭⲏ   ·ϯ·ⲧⲕⲁⲥ
-one   among-them   ()thirsting;   > and   did-my-soul   give-pain

ⲉⲭⲛ̅·ⲛ̅·ϣⲏⲣⲉ   ⲛ̅·ⲡ̅·ⲣⲱⲙⲉ   ⲭⲉ   2ⲛ̅·ⲃⲗⲗⲉⲉⲩ-
over-the-sons   of-men,   for   ()blind-me-

-ⲉ   ⲛⲉ   2ⲙ̅·ⲡⲟⲩ·2ⲏⲧ·ˋ   ⲁⲩⲱ   ⲥⲉ·ⲛⲁⲩ   ⲉⲃⲟⲗ   ⲁⲛ
-n (they) are   in-their-mind,   and   they-look   outward   not,

ⲭⲉ   ⲛ̅ⲧⲁⲩ·ⲉⲓ   ⲉ·ⲡ·ⲕⲟⲥⲙⲟⲥ   ⲉⲩ·ϣⲟⲩⲉⲓⲧ·ˋ   ⲉⲩ·
for   they-have-come   to-the-world   ()-empty;   they-

·ϣⲓⲛⲉ   ⲟⲛ   ⲉⲧⲣⲟⲩ·ⲉⲓ   ⲉⲃⲟⲗ   2ⲙ̅·ⲡ·ⲕⲟⲥⲙⲟⲥ
-seek   also   that-they-come   out   of-the-world

ⲉⲩ·ϣⲟⲩⲉⲓⲧ·ˋ   ⲡⲗⲏⲛ   ⲧⲉⲛⲟⲩ   ⲥⲉ·ⲧⲟ2ⲉ   2ⲟ-
()-empty;   > but   now   they-are-drunk;   wh-

-ⲧⲁⲛ   ⲉⲩ·ϣⲁⲛ·ⲛⲉ2·ⲡⲟⲩ·ⲏⲣⲡ·ˋ   ⲧⲟⲧⲉ   ⲥⲉ·ⲛⲁ·ⲣ̄·
-en   they-should-shakeoff-their-wine,   then   they-will-

·ⲙⲉⲧⲁⲛⲟⲉⲓ
-repent.

Jesus said, "I took my place in the midst of the world, and I appeared to them in flesh. I found all of them intoxicated; I found none of them thirsty. And my soul became afflicted for the sons of men, because they are blind in their hearts and do not have sight; for empty they came into the world, and empty too they seek to leave the world. But for the moment they are intoxicated. When they shake off their wine, then they will repent."

In this saying, Jesus refers to

Psalms 107:27-28

"They reel to and fro, and stagger like a drunken man, and are at their wits' end. Then they cry out to the Lord in their trouble, and He brings them out of their distresses."

We also find an analogous reference in

Matthew 13:13-14

"Therefore, I speak to them in parables, because seeing they do not see, and hearing they do not hear, nor do they understand. And in them the prophecy of Isaiah is fulfilled, which says: 'Hearing you will hear and shall not understand and seeing you will see and not perceive; for the hearts of this people have grown dull. Their ears are hard of hearing, and their eyes they have closed, lest they should see with their eyes and hear with their ears, lest they should understand with their hearts and turn, so that I should heal them.'"

29

ПЄХЄ·ĪC	<>	ЄϢХЄ	ÑТА·Т·САРΣ`
Said Jesus	(this)	If	has-the-flesh

·ϢШПЄ	ЄТВЄ·П̄ПА	ОУ·ϢПНРЄ	ТЄ	ЄϢ-
-come-into-being	because-of-spirit,	a-wonder	is-she;	> i-

-ХЄ·П̄ПА	ΔЄ	ЄТВЄ·П·CШМА	ОУ·ϢПНРЄ
-f-spirit,	hwvr,	because-of-the-body,	a-wonder

Ñ·ϢПНРЄ	ПЄ	АЛЛА	АNО·К`	†·Р̄·ϢПНРЄ
wonderous	is-he;	> Rather,	I,	I-become-amazed

М̄·ПАЄІ	ХЄ	ПШ[C]	А·[ТЄЄІ·]NОб	М̄·МN̄Т·РМ̄·МА-
at-this,	that	how	this-great	rich-

-О	АC·ОУШ2	2N̄·ТЄЄІ·МN̄Т·2НКЄ
-ness,	she-was-placed	in-this-poverty.

Jesus said, "If the flesh came into being because of spirit, it is a wonder. But if spirit came into being because of the body, it is a wonder of wonders. Indeed, I am amazed at how this great wealth has made its home in this poverty."

INTERPRETATION:

The saying illustrates an idea that is totally against Gnosticism. This philosophy affirms that Jesus did not come in the flesh but only in the Spirit and that the physical or bodily dimension is subject to corruption without the possibility of redemption. In this case, 'the poverty,' referring to the physical body, experiences the resurrection, which is 'the marvelous wonder.'

Jesus came in the flesh in Mary's womb, begotten by the Holy Spirit. In other words, the flesh came into being because of the Spirit.

"The spirit coming into being due to a bodily cause" speaks of the resurrection. The Spirit descends into Jesus' dead body and quickens it. It's a marvelous wonder. Heaven's eternal life intervened in this limited dimension subject to death.

This perspective is analogous to

> **2 Corinthians 4:7**
> "But we have this treasure in earthen vessels, that the excellence of the power may be of God and not of us."

30

пехе·їс
Said Jesus

хе	п·мА	еүῡ·Ϣомт	ῡ·ноүте	ῦ·мАү	2ῡ·
this:	the-place	which-has-three	gods	there,	in-

·ноүте	не	п·мА	еүῡ·снАү	н оүА	Ано·к`
-god	they-are;	> the-place	which-has-two	or one,	I,

†·ϣооп`	нммА·ϥ`
I-exist	with-him.

Jesus said, "Where there are three gods, they are gods. Where there are two or one, I am with him."

INTERPRETATION:

Indeed, God's distinctive feature is oneness. He is one: Father, Son, and Holy Spirit (Elohim).

The phrase "Where there is only one, I say that I am with him" is connected directly to us. Therefore "the One" refers to the wholeness of our being. When our heart and mind operate in oneness, and they are truly connected to God's Spirit.

31

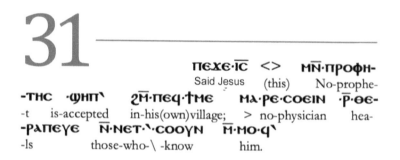

ΠⲈⲬⲈ·ⲒⲤ <> ⲘⲚ·ⲠⲢⲞΦⲎ-
Said Jesus (this) No-prophe-
-ⲦⲎⲤ ·ⲰⲎⲠ` ϨⲘ·ⲠⲈϥ·ⲦⲘⲈ ⲘⲀ·ⲢⲈ·ⲤⲞⲈⲒⲚ ·Ⲣ̄·ⲐⲈ-
-t is-accepted in-his(own)village; > no-physician hea-
-ⲢⲀⲠⲈⲨⲈ Ⲛ̄·ⲚⲈⲦ·`·ⲤⲞⲞⲨⲚ Ⲙ̄·ⲘⲞ·ϥ`
-ls those-who-\ -know him.

Jesus said, "No prophet is accepted in his own village; no physician heals those who know him."

INTERPRETATION:

This saying is analogous to

Luke 4:24
"Then He said, "Assuredly, I say to you, no prophet is accepted in his own country.""

The heart tends to refuse to believe someone extraordinary could be close to us. We show greater appreciation for those coming from the outside.

32

ⲭⲉ	ⲟⲩ·ⲡⲟⲗⲓⲥ	ⲉⲩ·ⲕⲱⲧ	ⲙ̄·ⲙⲟ·ⲥ	ϩⲓⲭⲛ̄·ⲟⲩ·ⲧⲟ-
this:	a-city	they-are-building	(her)	upon-a-moun-

-ⲟⲩ	ⲉϥ·ϫⲟⲥⲉ	ⲉⲥ·ⲧⲁⲭⲣⲏⲩ	ⲙⲛ̄·ϭⲟⲙ	ⲛ̄ⲥ·ϩⲉ
-tain	()raised-up,	she-being-fortified,	no-way	that-she-fall

ⲟⲩⲇⲉ	ⲥ·ⲛⲁϣ·ϩⲱⲡˋ	ⲁⲛ
&nor	she-can-be-hidden	not.

Jesus said, "A city being built on a high mountain and fortified cannot fall, nor can it be hidden."

INTERPRETATION:

The verse is analogous to

Matthew 5:14
"You are the light of the world. A city that is set on a hill cannot be hidden."

In this case, it speaks of the city of the living God, seated on Mount Zion in heaven and fortified by God's inexpugnable presence.

ΠⲈⲬⲈ·ⲒC <> ΠⲈⲦ·`·Ⲕ·ⲚⲀ·
Said Jesus :his) he-who\you(sg)-will

·ⲤⲰⲦⲘ̄ ⲈⲢⲞ·Ϥ Ⲥ̄Ⲙ̄·ΠⲈⲔ·`·ⲘⲀⲀⲬⲈ Ⲥ̄Ⲙ̄·Π·ⲔⲈ·ⲘⲀ-
-listen to-him in-your(sg)- \ -ear (and?) in-the-other-ea

-ⲀⲬⲈ ·ⲦⲀϢⲈ·ⲞⲈⲒϢ` Ⲙ̄·ⲘⲞ·Ϥ ⲤⲒⲬⲚ̄·ⲚⲈⲦⲚ̄·ⲬⲈ-
-r, preach him upon-your(pl)-ho·

-ⲚⲈΠⲰⲢ` ⲘⲀ·ⲢⲈ·ⲖⲀⲀⲨ` ⲄⲀⲢ ·ⲬⲈⲢⲈ·Ⲥ̄Ⲏ̄ⲂⲤ̄ Ⲛ̄Ϥ·`
-usetops; >(for) does-not-anyone, (---), burn(a)lamp &()-

·ⲔⲀⲀ·Ϥ` Ⲥ̄Ⲁ·ⲘⲀⲀⲬⲈ ⲞⲨⲆⲈ ⲘⲀϤ·ⲔⲀⲀ·Ϥ` Ⲥ̄Ⲙ̄·ⲘⲀ
-put-him under-ear(?) &nor does-not-he-put-him in(a)place

ⲈϤ·ⲤⲎΠ` ⲀⲖⲖⲀ Ⲉ·ϢⲀⲢⲈϤ·ⲔⲀⲀ·Ϥ` ⲤⲒⲬⲚ̄·Ⲧ·ⲀⲨ-
()hidden. >Rather, does-he-put-him upon-the-lamp

-ⲬⲚⲒⲀ ⲬⲈⲔⲀⲀⲤ ⲞⲨⲞⲚ ·ⲚⲒⲘ` ⲈⲦ·ⲂⲎⲔ` Ⲉ·Ⲥ̄ⲞⲨⲚ
-stand, sothat one -any who-goes in

ⲀⲨⲰ ⲈⲦ·Ⲛ̄ⲚⲎⲨ ⲈⲂⲞⲖ ⲈⲨ·ⲚⲀ·ⲚⲀⲨ Ⲁ·ΠⲈϤ·ⲞⲨ-
and who-comes out, they-may-look upon-his-li-

-ⲞⲈⲒⲚ
-ght.

Jesus said, "Preach from your (pl.) housetops that which you (sg.) will hear in your (sg.) ear. For no one lights a lamp and puts it under a bushel, nor does he put it in a hidden place, but rather he sets it on a lampstand so that everyone who enters and leaves will see its light."

INTERPRETATION:

This verse is analogous to

Matthew 10:27 and Luke 12:3

"Whatever I tell you in the dark, speak in the light; and what you hear in the ear, preach on the housetops."

It's also similar to

Matthew 5:15

"Nor do they light a lamp and put it under a basket, but on a lampstand, and it gives light to all who are in the house."

34

ΠЄΧЄ·ĪC ΚЄ ΟΥ·ΒⲖⲖЄ   ЄϤ·ϢⲀⲚ·ˋ·ⲤⲰⲔˋ
Said Jesus this: a-blindman, if-he-should-\-lead
ⲒⲎⲦ·Ϥˋ   Ⲛ·ⲚΟΥ·ΒⲖⲖЄ   ϢⲀΥ·ⲀЄ   Ⲙ·ΠЄ·ⲤⲚⲀΥˋ
before-him   a-blind-man,   they-fall,   the-two,
Є·Π·ЄⲤ𝐇Τˋ   Є·Υ·ⲀⲒЄⲒΤˋ
down   into-a-pit.

Jesus said, "If a blind man leads a blind man, they will both fall into a pit."

INTERPRETATION:

This verse is analogous to

Matthew 15:14

"Let them alone. They are blind leaders of the blind. And if the blind leads the blind, both will fall into a ditch," referring to the Pharisees.

35

ΠΕΧΕ·ΙC	<>	ΜΝ·6ΟΜ˙
Said Jesus	(this)	no-way

ΝΤΕ·ΟΥΑ	·ΒΩΚ˙	Ε2ΟΥΝ	Ε·Π·ΗΕΙ	Μ·Π·ΧΩ-
can-one	go	in	to-the-house	of-the-str-

-ΩΡΕ	Νϥ·ΧΙΤ·ϥ˙	Ν·ΧΝΑ2	ΕΙΜΗΤΙ	Νϥ·ΜΟΥΡ
-ong	&()-take-him	by-force,	unless	()he-bind

Ν·ΝΕϥ·6ΙΧ˙	>	ΤΟΤΕ	ϥ·ΝΑ·ΠΩΩΝΕ	ΕΒΟΛ
his-hands;		then	he-will-move	out

Μ·ΠΕϥ·ΗΕΙ
of-his-house.

Jesus said, "It is not possible for anyone to enter the house of a strong man and take it by force unless he binds his hands; then he will (be able to) ransack his house."

INTERPRETATION:

This passage is analogous to

Mark 3:27

"No one can enter a strong man's house and plunder his goods unless he first binds the strong man. And then he will plunder his house."

As for spiritual warfare, it is a foundation. Some battles feature a strong man, which we must bind before plundering the house.

36

ΠΕΧΕ·ΙC	<>	Μ̄Ν·ϥΙ·ΡΟΟΥϢ	ΧΙ ̄·
Said Jesus	(this)	Do-not-take-care	from-

·2ΤΟΟΥΕ	ϢΑ·ΡΟΥ2Ε	ΑΥϢ	ΧΙΝ·2Ι·ΡΟΥ2Ε
-morning	upto-evening,	and	from()evening

ϢΑ·2ΤΟΟΥΕ	ΧΕ	ΟΥ	ΠΕ	ΕΤ·ΝΑ·ΤΑΑ·ϥ	2ΙϢΤ·˅
up-to-morning	for	what	(it) is	which-will-give-him	upon-\

·ΤΗΥΤ̄Ν
-yourselves. >

Jesus said, "Do not be concerned from morning until evening and from evening until morning about what you will wear."

INTERPRETATION:

This passage is analogous with

 Matthew 6:25-34

"That is why I tell you not to worry about everyday life—whether you have enough food and drink or enough clothes to wear. Isn't life more than food, and your body more than clothing? Look at the birds. They don't plant or harvest or store food in barns, for your heavenly Father feeds them. And aren't you far more valuable to him than they are? Can all your worries add a single moment to your life? And why worry about your clothing? Look at the lilies of the field and how they grow. They don't work or make their clothing, yet Solomon in all his glory was not dressed as beautifully as they are. And if God cares so wonderfully for wildflowers that are here today and thrown into the fire tomorrow, he will certainly care for you. Why do you have so little faith? So, don't worry about these things, saying, 'What will we eat? What will we drink? What will we wear?' These things dominate the thoughts of unbelievers, but your heavenly Father already knows all your needs. Seek the Kingdom of God above all else, and live righteously, and he will give you everything you need. So don't worry about tomorrow, for tomorrow will bring its own worries. Today's trouble is enough for today."

37

ΠΕΧΕ·ΝΕϥ·ΜΑΘΗΤΗϹ ΧΕ ΑϢ Ν̄·
Said-his-disciples this: which -

·Ⲍ̄ΟΟΥ ΕΚ·ΝΑ·ΟΥⲰΝⲌ̄ ΕΒΟⲖ ΝΑ·Ν ΑΥⲰ ΑϢ
-day will-you(sg)-appear forth to-us? And which

Ν̄·Ⲍ̄ΟΟΥ ΕΝΑ·ΝΑΥ ΕΡΟ·Κ` ΠΕΧΕ·Ι̅Ϲ̅ ΧΕ ⲌΟ-
day will-we-look upon-you(sg)? *Said-JS37 this: Wh-

-ΤΑΝ ΕΤΕΤΝ̄·ϢΑ·ΚΕΚ·ΘΥΤΝ̄ Ε·ⲌΗΥ Μ̄ΠΕ-
-en you(pl)-should-strip-yourselves naked without-be-

-ΤΝ̄·ϢΙΠΕ ΑΥⲰ Ν̄ΤΕΤΝ̄·ϤΙ Ν̄·ΝΕΤΝ̄·ϢΤΗΝ
-ing-ashamed, and ()-you(pl)-take your(pl)-garments

Ν̄ΤΕΤΝ̄·ΚΑΑ·Υ ⲌΑ·Π·ΕϹΗΤ` Ν̄·ΝΕΤΝ̄·ΟΥΕΡΗ-
&-you(pl)-put-them under-the-ground of-your(pl)-fee-

-ΤΕ Ν̄·ΘΕ Ν̄·ΝΙ·ΚΟΥΕΙ Ν̄·ϢΗΡΕ·ϢΗΜ` Ν̄ΤΕ-
-t, like those-little small-children, &-you-

-ΤΝ̄·ΧΟΠΧΠ̄` Μ̄·ΜΟ·ΟΥ ΤΟΤ[Ε ΤΕΤΝΑ·ΝΑ]Υ
-(pl)-trample them, > then you(pl)-will-look

Ε·Π·ϢΗΡΕ Μ̄·ΠΕΤ·ΟΝⲌ ΑΥⲰ ΤΕΤΝΑ·Ρ̄·
upon-the-son of-he-who-lives, and you(pl)-will-become-

·ⲌΟΤΕ ΑΝ
-afraid not.

His disciples said, "When will you become revealed to us and when shall we see you?" Jesus said, "When you disrobe without being ashamed and take up your garments and place them under your feet like little children and tread on them, then [will you see] the son of the living one, and you will not be afraid."

INTERPRETATION:

There is a story of Francis of Assisi, who, to become a follower of Jesus Christ, stripped himself of his garments, remaining naked in front of Assisi society. He did this in both a spiritual and physical sense, to leave behind any expectation of being a young heir to his family's wealth. Thus, he left behind his identity to begin his path to becoming "Francis," a son of God, whom the garments of his society and time will no longer define. He didn't find in who he was anything to cling to, and in the likeness of the Son of God, he emptied himself as children do, naked but clothed by God.

The example set forth by Francis speaks for itself. In a spiritual sense, we must divest ourselves of what serves to cover or protect us other than God.

38

ΠΕΧΕ·ΙC ΧΕ ΖΑΖ Ν̄·ϹΟΠ ΑΤΕΤΝ̄·
Said Jesus this: Many times did-you(pl)·

·P̄·ΕΠΙΘΥΜΕΙ Ε·ϹШΤΜ̄ Α·ΝΕΕΙ·ШΑΧΕ ΝΑΕΙ
-become-desirous to-listen to-these-words, these

ΕΤ·ΧШ Μ̄·ΜΟ·ΟΥ ΝΗ·ΤΝ̄ ΑΥШ ΜΝ̄·ΤΗ·ΤΝ̄·
which-I-speak them to-you(pl), and not-have-you(pl)·

·ΚΕ·ΟΥΑ Ε·ϹΟΤΜ·ΟΥ Ν̄·ΤΟΟΤ·Q̄ ΟΥΝ̄·ΖΝ̄·ΖΟ-
-another-one to-hear-them from-his-hand. > ()some-da-

-ΟΥ ·ΝΑ·ШШΠΕ Ν̄ΤΕΤΝ̄·ШΙΝΕ Ν̄ϹШ·ΕΙ ΤΕ-
-ys will-come-to-be &-you(pl)(will)seek after-me; you-

-ΤΝΑ·ΖΕ ΑΝ ΕΡΟ·ΕΙ
-(pl)-will-fall not upon-me.

Jesus said, "Many times have you desired to hear these words which I am saying to you, and you

have no one else to hear them from. There will be days when you will look for me and will not find me."

INTERPRETATION:

The verse is analogous to

John 6:68
"But Simon Peter answered Him, "Lord, to whom shall we go? You have the words of eternal life."

Our spirit seeks nourishment of eternal substance. In essence, the Word made flesh come down to open that source of eternal life in us — the possibility of the Word of God dwelling in us, which was only fulfilled following his death and resurrection.

John 16:16-24 provides us with a deeper perspective:

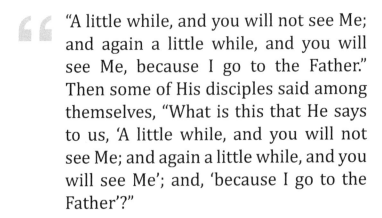

"A little while, and you will not see Me; and again a little while, and you will see Me, because I go to the Father." Then some of His disciples said among themselves, "What is this that He says to us, 'A little while, and you will not see Me; and again a little while, and you will see Me'; and, 'because I go to the Father'?"

They said therefore, "What is this that He says, 'A little while'? We do not know what He is saying." Now Jesus knew that they desired to ask Him, and He said to them, "Are you inquiring among yourselves about what I said, 'A little while, and you will not see Me; and again a little while, and you will see Me'? Most assuredly, I say to you that you will weep and lament, but the world will rejoice; and you will be sorrowful, but your sorrow will be turned into joy.

A woman, when she is in labor, has sorrow because her hour has come; but as soon as she has given birth to the child, she no longer remembers the anguish for joy that a human being has been born into the world. Therefore, you now have sorrow; but I will see you again and your heart will rejoice, and your joy no one will take from you. "And on that day you will ask Me nothing. Most assuredly, I say to you, whatever you ask the Father in My name He will give you. Until now you have asked nothing in My name. Ask, and you will receive, that your joy may be full."

39

πεχε·ῑⲤ χε ⲙ·φαρισαι-
Said Jesus this: the-Pharisee-

-ⲟⲥ ⲙⲛ·ⲛ·ⲅⲣⲁⲙⲙⲁⲧⲉⲩⲥ ⲁⲩ·χι ⲛ·ϣⲁϣⲧ`
-s and-the-scribes, they-took the-keys

ⲛ·ⲧ·ⲅⲛⲱⲥⲓⲥ ⲁⲩ·ϩⲟⲡ·ⲟⲩ ⲟⲩⲧⲉ ⲙ̄ⲡⲟⲩ·ⲃⲱⲕ`
of-Knowledge; they-hid-them; > -nor did-not-they-go

ⲉϩⲟⲩⲛ ⲁⲩⲱ ⲛⲉⲧ·ⲟⲩⲱϣ ⲉ·ⲃⲱⲕ` ⲉϩⲟⲩⲛ ⲙ̄-
in, and those-who-desire to-go in, did-not-

-ⲡⲟⲩ·ⲕⲁⲁ·ⲩ ⲛ̄·ⲧⲱ·ⲧⲛ̄ ⲇⲉ ·ϣⲱⲡⲉ ⲙ̄·ⲫⲣⲟⲛⲓⲙⲟⲥ
-they-permit-them. > You(pl), hwvr, come-to-be cunning,

ⲛ̄·ⲑⲉ ⲛ̄·ⲛ·ϩⲟϥ` ⲁⲩⲱ ⲛ̄·ⲁⲕⲉⲣⲁⲓⲟⲥ ⲛ̄·ⲑⲉ ⲛ̄·ⲛ·
like the-snakes, and innocent, like the-

·ϭⲣⲟⲙⲡⲉ
-doves.

Jesus said, "The pharisees and the scribes have taken the keys of knowledge (gnosis) and hidden them. They themselves have not entered, nor have they allowed to enter those who wish to. You, however, be as wise as serpents and as innocent as doves."

INTERPRETATION:

This saying is analogous to

> **Matthew 23:13**
> "But woe to you, scribes and Pharisees, hypocrites! For you shut up the kingdom of heaven against men; for you neither go in yourselves, nor do you allow those who are entering to go in."

> And also to **Luke 11:52**
> "Woe to you lawyers! For you have

taken away the key of knowledge. You did not enter in yourselves, and those who were entering in you hindered."

40

ⲡⲉⲝⲉ·ⲓ̄ⲥ̄ <> ⲟⲩ·ⲃⲉ·ⲛ·ⲉⲗⲟⲟⲗⲉ ⲁⲩ·
Said Jesus (this) a-vine-of-grapes, did-they-
·ⲧⲟϭ·ⲥ ⲙ̄·ⲡ·ⲥⲁ·ⲛ·ⲃⲟⲗ ⲙ̄·ⲡ·ⲉⲓⲱⲧˋ ⲁⲩⲱ ⲉⲥ·ⲧⲁ-
-plant-her in-the-side-outer of-the-father, > and she-being-for-
-ⲭⲣⲏⲩ ⲁⲛ ⲥⲉ·ⲛⲁ·ⲡⲟⲣⲕ·ⲥ̄ ϩⲁ·ⲧⲉⲥ·ⲛⲟⲩⲛⲉ ⲛ̄ⲥ·
-tified not, they-will-pull-her-up by-her-root &-she(will)-
·ⲧⲁⲕⲟ
-be-destroyed.

Jesus said, "A grapevine has been planted outside of the Father, but being unsound, it will be pulled up by its roots and destroyed."

INTERPRETATION:

The passage closely parallels the song of the vineyard, prophesied by Isaiah, and it refers to Israel's apostasy.

Isaiah 5:1-7
"Now let me sing to my Well-beloved a song of my beloved regarding His vineyard. My Well-beloved has a vineyard on a very fruitful hill. He dug it up and cleared out its stones and planted it with the choicest vine. He built a tower in its midst, and also made

a winepress in it, so He expected it to bring forth good grapes, but it brought forth wild grapes.

"And now, O inhabitants of Jerusalem and men of Judah, Judge, please, between Me and My vineyard. What more could have been done to My vineyard that I have not done in it? Why then, when I expected it to bring forth good grapes, did it bring forth wild grapes? And now, please let Me tell you what I will do to My vineyard: I will take away its hedge, and it shall be burned; and break down its wall, and it shall be trampled down.

I will lay it to waste. It shall not be pruned or dug, but there shall come up briers and thorns. I will also command the clouds

That they rain no rain on it. For the vineyard of the Lord of hosts is the house of Israel, and the men of Judah are His pleasant plant. He looked for justice, but behold, oppression;

For righteousness, but behold, a cry for help."

41

ⲡⲉϫⲉ·ⲓⲥ ϫⲉ ⲡⲉⲧ·ⲉⲩⲛ̄·ⲧⲁ·ϥ ⲑⲛ̄·ⲧⲉϥ·
Said Jesus this: he-who-has-it/he in-his-
·ϭⲓϫ ⲥⲉ·ⲛⲁ·ⲧ ⲛⲁ·ϥ ⲁⲩⲱ ⲡⲉⲧⲉ·ⲙⲛ̄·ⲧⲁ·ϥ ⲡ·ⲕⲉ·
-hand, they-will-give to-him, > and he-who-has-not(it), the-other-
·ϣⲏⲙ ⲉⲧ·ⲟⲩⲛ̄·ⲧⲁ·ϥ ⲥⲉ·ⲛⲁ·ϥⲓⲧ·ϥ̄ ⲛ̄·ⲧⲟⲟⲧ·ϥ
-little-bit which-has-he, they-will-take-it(m) from-his-hand.

Jesus said, "Whoever has something in his hand will receive more, and whoever has nothing will be deprived of even the little he has."

INTERPRETATION:

This verse is analogous to

Luke 8:18

"Therefore, take heed how you hear. For whoever has, to him more will be given; and whoever does not have, even what he seems to have will be taken from him."

(similar to **Matthew 13:12, Matthew 25:29, Mark 4:25, Luke 19:26**)

Far from being an unjust God, He is a loving father who sees His DNA in His children. He was the One who endowed us with abundance, fullness, and possibilities in everything. We must now recognize the never-ending resources within us and not allow a mindset of lack, limitations, slothfulness, and indifference since it can easily blind us to God's provision.

On the contrary, knowing how to manage everything, He entrusts us with properly allows us to receive even more.

He who does not give is a poor steward of God's resources and will be stripped of possessions to hand over to one who can administer in the righteousness of the Kingdom.

42

ΠЄХЄ·ΙC	ХЄ	·ϢϢΠЄ	ЄТЄТΝ·Р·ΠΑΡΑΓЄ
Said Jesus	this:	come-into-being	as-you(pl)-pass-away.

Jesus said, "Become passers-by."

INTERPRETATION:

Our victory lies in knowing that everything visible is subject to God's invisible Kingdom and responds to the substance of faith "so that the things which are seen were made out of that which is not seen." (Hebrews 11:3)

These words go hand in hand with what is written in **2 Corinthians 4:18**

 "...while we do not look at the things which are seen, but at the things which are not seen. For the things which are seen are temporary, but the things which are not seen are eternal."

Becoming passers-by is to be sure that the eternal and unshakable rules over circumstances and situation to pass through them untroubled.

This was precisely Abraham's attitude, who, though having everything in this world, lived as a foreigner.

 Hebrews 11:8-10
"By faith Abraham obeyed when he was called to go out to the place which he would receive as an inheritance. And he went out, not knowing where he was going. By faith he dwelt in the land of promise as in a foreign country, dwelling in tents with Isaac and Jacob, the heirs with him of the same promise; for he waited for the city which has foundations, whose builder and maker is God."

43

ⲡⲉⲝⲉ·ⲓ̄ⲥ ⲝⲉ ·ⲱⲱⲡⲉ ⲉⲧⲉⲧⲛ̄·ⲣ̄·ⲡⲁⲣⲁⲅⲉ
Said Jesus this: come-into-being as-you(pl)-pass-away.

ⲡⲉⲝⲁ·ⲩ ⲛⲁ·ϥ ⲛ̄ϭⲓ·ⲛⲉϥ·`·ⲙⲁⲑⲏⲧⲏⲥ ⲝⲉ ⲛ̄·ⲧⲁ·ⲕ
Said-they to-him, viz-his- \ -disciples, this: You(sg)(are)

ⲛⲓⲙ ⲉⲕ·ⲝⲱ ⲛ̄·ⲛⲁⲓ̈ ⲛⲁ·ⲛ ϩⲛ̄·ⲛⲉⲧ·ⲝⲱ ⲙ̄·
who, that-you(sg)-speak these(things) to-us? > In-those-which-I-speak

·ⲙⲟ·ⲟⲩ ⲛⲏ·ⲧⲛ̄ ⲛ̄ⲧⲉⲧⲛ̄·ⲉⲓⲙⲉ ⲁⲛ ⲝⲉ ⲁⲛⲟ·ⲕ
-them to-you(pl), ()you(pl)-realize not that I (am)

ⲛⲓⲙ ⲁⲗⲗⲁ ⲛ̄·ⲧⲱ·ⲧⲛ̄ ⲁⲧⲉⲧⲛ̄·ⲱⲱⲡⲉ ⲛ̄·ⲑⲉ ⲛ̄·
who; > Rather, you(pl), have-you(pl)-come-to-be like -

·ⲛⲓ·ⲓ̈ⲟⲩⲇⲁⲓⲟⲥ ⲝⲉ ⲥⲉ·ⲙⲉ ⲙ̄·ⲡ·ⲱⲏⲛ ⲥⲉ·ⲙⲟⲥ·
-those-Judeans, for they-love the-tree, they-ha-

·ⲧⲉ ⲙ̄·ⲡⲉϥ·ⲕⲁⲣⲡⲟⲥ ⲁⲩⲱ ⲥⲉ·ⲙⲉ ⲙ̄·ⲡ·ⲕⲁⲣⲡⲟⲥ
-te his-fruit, and they-love the-fruit,

ⲥⲉ·ⲙⲟⲥⲧⲉ ⲙ̄·ⲡ·ⲱⲏⲛ
they-hate the-tree.

His disciples said to him, "Who are you, that you should say these things to us?" <Jesus said to them,> "You do not realize who I am from what I say to you, but you have become like the Jews, for they (either) love the tree and hate its fruit (or) love the fruit and hate the tree."

INTERPRETATION:

Jesus refers to the hypocrisy of the Pharisees and warns his disciples not to fall for it, making it clear that to receive him is to receive his words. Jesus is the tree, and his fruit is the righteousness that comes by faith, the life of miracles, and heaven's abundance.

In contrast, the Jews of his time claimed to love God but despised his Son.

44

ΠⲈϪⲈ·ⲒⲤ ϪⲈ ΠⲈⲦⲀ·ϪⲈ·
Said Jesus this: whoever-tells-

·ⲞⲨⲀ Ⲁ·Π·ⲈⲒⲰⲦ` ⲤⲈ·ⲚⲀ·ⲔⲰ ⲈⲂⲞⲖ ⲚⲀ·Ϥ` ⲀⲨⲰ
-one to-the-father, they-will-leave off to-him, > and

ΠⲈⲦⲀ·ϪⲈ·ⲞⲨⲀ Ⲉ·Π·ϢⲎⲢⲈ ⲤⲈ·ⲚⲀ·ⲔⲰ ⲈⲂⲞⲖ
whoever-tells-one to-the-son, they-will-leave off

ⲚⲀ·Ϥ` ΠⲈⲦⲀ·ϪⲈ·ⲞⲨⲀ ⲆⲈ Ⲁ·Π·ΠⲚⲀ ⲈⲦ·ⲞⲨⲀⲀⲂ
to-him; > whoever-tells-one, hwvr, to-the-spirit which-is-holy,

ⲤⲈ·ⲚⲀ·ⲔⲰ ⲀⲚ ⲈⲂⲞⲖ ⲚⲀ·Ϥ` ⲞⲨⲦⲈ Ⲋ̅Ⲙ·Π·ⲔⲀⲊ
they-will-leave not off to-him, n/nor on-the-earth

ⲞⲨⲦⲈ Ⲋ̅Ⲛ·Ⲧ·ΠⲈ
n/nor in-the-sky.

Jesus said, "Whoever blasphemes against the father will be forgiven, and whoever blasphemes against the son will be forgiven, but whoever blasphemes against the holy spirit will not be forgiven either on earth or in heaven."

INTERPRETATION:

This passage is analogous to

Mark 3:28-29

"Assuredly, I say to you, all sins will be forgiven the sons of men, and whatever blasphemies they may utter; but he who blasphemes against the Holy Spirit never has forgiveness but is subject to eternal condemnation."

45

ΠΕΧΕ·ῙC̄ <> ΜΑΥ·ΧΕΛΕ·ΕΛΟΟ-
Said Jesus (this) do-not-they-harvest-grap-

-ΛΕ ΕΒΟΛ 2Ν·ϢΟΝΤΕ ΟΥΤΕ ΜΑΥ·ΚϢΤϤ·ˋ
-es out of-thorns -nor do-not-they-gather-

·ΚΝ̄ΤΕ ΕΒΟΛ 2Ν̄·CΡ̄·ϬΑΜΟΥΛˋ ΜΑΥ·†·ΚΑΡΠΟC
-figs out of-(thistles); (for) do-not-they-give-fruit

[ΓΑΡ ΟΥ·ΑΓΑ]ΘΟC Ρ̄·ΡϢΜΕ ϢΑϤ·ΕΙΝΕ Ν̄·
(---). > A-good man, does-he-bring -

·ΟΥ·ΑΓΑΘΟΝ ΕΒΟΛ 2[Μ̄·]ΠΕϤ·Ε2Ο ΟΥ·ΚΑ[ΚΟC]
-a-good-thing out of-his-treasure; > an-evil

Ρ̄·ΡϢΜΕ ϢΑϤ·ΕΙΝΕ Ν̄·2Ν̄·ΠΟΝΗΡΟΝ ΕΒΟΛ
man, does-he-bring some-evil-things out

2Μ̄·ΠΕϤ·Ε2Ο ΕΘΟΟΥ ΕΤ·2Ν̄·ΠΕϤ·2ΗΤˋ ΑΥ-
of-his-treasure which-is-wicked, which-is-in-his-mind, an-

-Ϣ Ν̄Ϥ·ΧϢ Ν̄·2Ν̄·ΠΟΝΗΡΟΝ ΕΒΟΛ ΓΑΡ 2Μ̄·
-d ()he-speaks some-evil-things, > (for) out, (---), of-

·ΦΟΥΟ Μ̄·ΦΗΤˋ ϢΑϤ·ˋ·ΕΙΝΕ ΕΒΟΛ Ν̄·2Ν̄·ΠΟ-
-the-excess of-the-mind, does-he-\-bring out some-evil-

-ΝΗΡΟΝ
-things.

Jesus said, "Grapes are not harvested from thorns, nor are figs gathered from thistles, for they do not produce fruit. A good man brings forth good from his storehouse; an evil man brings forth evil things from his evil storehouse, which is in his heart, and says evil things. For out of the abundance of the heart he brings forth evil things."

INTERPRETATION:

This passage is analogous to

Luke 6:45

"A good man out of the good treasure of his heart brings forth good; and an evil man out of the evil treasure of

his heart brings forth evil. For out of the abundance of the heart his mouth speaks."

46

πεχε·ιc χε χιn·\·αλαμ ϣα·ΐω2α -
Said Jesus this: From-\-Adam, upto-Johan-
-nhc π·βαπτιcτhc 2ν·ν·χπο ν·ν·2ιομε
-nes the-Baptist, among-the-begotten of-women,
μν·πετ·χοcε α·ΐω2αννhc π·βαπτι-
no-one-who-is-raised-up above-Johann the-Bapti-
-cthc ϣιnα χε ν·ογωόπ' νόι·νεq·βαλ
-st, so that to-break(lower) viz-his-eyes;
αει·χο·οc λε χε πετ·nα·ϣωπε 2ν·thγ-
I-spoke, hwvr, this- he-who-will-come-to-be among-you-
-tν εq·ο ν·κογει q·nα·cογων·t·μnτε-
-(pl), he-being a-little-one, he-will-know-the-kingd-
-πο αγω q·nα·χιcε α·ΐω2αννhc
-om, and he-will-be-raised-up above-Johann.

Jesus said, "Among those born of women, from Adam until John the Baptist, there is no one so superior to John the Baptist that his eyes should not be lowered (before him). Yet I have said, whichever one of you comes to be a child will be acquainted with the kingdom and will become superior to John."

INTERPRETATION:

This passage is analogous to

 Matthew 11:11

"Assuredly, I say to you, among those born of women there has not risen one greater than John the Baptist; but he

who is least in the kingdom of heaven
is greater than he."

The Kingdom of Heaven belongs to the children.
That pure and genuine faith qualifies to be even
greater than John. The simplicity of a child leaves
aside all human corruption of the longing to be
exalted.

It's an extraordinary promise that any little one
in the Kingdom is greater than all the prophets.

47

ΠΕΧΕ·ΙC
Said Jesus

ΧΕ	ΜΝ·6ΟΜ	ΝΤΕ·ΟΥ·ΡШΜΕ	·ΤΕλΟ	λ·2ΤΟ
this:	no-way	can-a-man	climb	onto-horses

CΝΑΥ	Νq·ΧШλΚ`	Μ·ΠΙΤΕ	·CΝΤΕ	λΥШ	ΜΝ·
two	&()-stretch	bows	-two(f), >	and	no-

·6ΟΜ`	ΝΤΕ·ΟΥ·2Μ2λλ	·ШΜШΕ·ΧΟΕΙC	·CΝΑΥ
-way	can-a-servant	serve-Lords	-two,

Η	q·ΝΑ·Ρ·ΤΙΜΑ	Μ·Π·ΟΥλ`	λΥШ	Π·ΚΕ·ΟΥλ	q·ΝΑ·
or	he-will-honor	the-one,	and	the-other-one,	he-will-

·Ρ·2ΥΒΡΙΖΕ	Μ·ΜΟ·q`	ΜΑ·ΡΕ·ΡШΜΕ	·CΕ·ΠΙΙ·ΑC
-despise	him. >	No-man	drinks-wine-old,

λΥШ	Ν·Τ·ΕΥΝΟΥ	Νq·`·ΕΠΙΘΥΜΕΙ	λ·CШ	ΗΡΠ`
and	immediately	(he)- \ -desires	to-drink	wine

Β·ΒΡΡΕ	λΥШ	ΜΑΥ·ΝΟΥΧ·`·ΗΡΠ`	Β·ΒΡΡΕ	Ε·ΑC-
new. >	And	they-do-not-pour-\ -wine	new	(in)to-wine-

-ΚΟC	Ν·ΑC	ΧΕΚλΑC	ΝΝΟΥ·ΠШ2	λΥШ	ΜΑΥ·
-skins	old,	sothat	they-not-split(open).	And	do-not-they-

·ΝΕΧ·`·ΗΡΠ`	Ν·ΑC	Ε·ΑCΚΟC	Β·ΒΡΡΕ	ШΙΝΑ	ΧΕ
-pour-\ -wine	old	into-wineskins	new,	so	that

ΝΕ·q·ΤΕΚλ·q`	ΜΑΥ·Χλ6·ΤΟΕΙC	Ν·ΑC	λ·ШΤΗ
he-destroy-him; >	they-do-not-sew-patches	old	to-garments

Ν·ШλΕΙ	ΕΠΕΙ	ΟΥΝ·ΟΥ·ΠШ2	·ΝΑ·ШШΠΕ
new,	because	there()-a-split	will-come-into-being.

Jesus said, "It is impossible for a man to mount two horses or to stretch two bows. And it is impossible for a servant to serve two masters; otherwise, he willhonor the one and treat the other contemptuously. No man drinks old wine and immediately desires to drink new wine. And new wine is not put into old wineskins, lest they burst; nor is old wine put into a new wineskin, lest it spoil it. An old patch is not sewn into a new garment, because a tear would result."

INTERPRETATION:

This passage is analogous to **Matthew 6:24**

 "No one can serve two masters; for either he will hate the one and love the other, or else he will be loyal to the one and despise the other. You cannot serve God and riches."

And also, with **Matthew 9:16-17**

 "No one puts a piece of unshrunk cloth on an old garment; for]the patch pulls away from the garment, and the tear is made worse. Nor do they put new wine into old wineskins or else the wineskins break, the wine is spilled, and the wineskins are ruined. But they put new wine into new wineskins, and both are preserved."

48

ⲡⲉⲭⲉ·ⲓ̅ⲥ̅	ⲭⲉ	ⲉⲣ ϣ ⲁ·ⲥⲛⲁⲩ	·ⲡ̅·ⲉⲓⲣⲏⲛⲏ	ⲙ̅ⲛ̅·
Said Jesus	this:	should-two	make-peace	with-

·ⲛⲟⲩ·ⲉⲣⲏⲩ	ϩ̅ⲙ̅·ⲡⲉⲓ·ⲏⲉⲓ	ⲟⲩ ⲱ ⲧ̀	ⲥⲉ·ⲛⲁ·ⲭⲟ·ⲟⲥ
-each-other	in-this-house	alone,	they-will-speak

ⲙ̅·ⲡ·ⲧⲁⲩ	ⲭⲉ	·ⲡ ⲱ ⲱ ⲛⲉ	ⲉⲃⲟ ⲗ	ⲁⲩ ⲱ	ϥ·ⲛⲁ·ⲧ ⲱ̅-
to-the(mountain?)	this-	"Move	away",	and	he-will-m-

-ⲱ ⲛⲉ
-ove.

Jesus said, "If two make peace with each other in this one house, they will say to the mountain, 'Move away,' and it will move away."

INTERPRETATION:

This passage is analogous to

Matthew 17:20

"So Jesus said to them, "Because of your unbelief; for assuredly, I say to you, if you have faith as a mustard seed, you will say to this mountain, 'Move from here to there,' and it will move; and nothing will be impossible for you.""

There is a fundamental truth here: the power of unity. Both within oneself united in mind and heart to the Spirit of God, and with being a united body of believers. It is in that unity, wherein lies the true power to remove every mountain of darkness.

49

ΠЄΧЄ·ĪC	ΧЄ	ЄΡϢΑ·CΝΑΥ	·Ρ·ЄΙΡΗΝΗ	ΜΝ·
Said Jesus	this:	should-two	make-peace	with-
·ΝΟΥ·ЄΡΗΥ	?Μ·ΠЄΙ·ΗЄΙ	ΟΥϢΤ˟	CЄ·ΝΑ·ΧΟ·ΟC	
-each-other	in-this-house	alone,	they-will-speak	
Μ·Π·ΤΑΥ	ΧЄ	·ΠϢϢΝЄ	ЄΒΟλ	ΑΥϢ	ϥ·ΝΑ·ΠϢ-
to-the(mountain?)	this-	"Move	away",	and	he-will-m-
-ϢΝЄ				
-ove.				

Jesus said, "Blessed are the solitary and elect, for you will find the kingdom. For you are from it, and to it you will return."

INTERPRETATION:

The same blessing is found in the description of those examples of faith in

Hebrews 11:38

"Of whom the world was not worthy. They wandered in deserts and mountains, in dens and caves of the earth."

The seal of God's eternity within us often leads us to paths not commonly traveled or understood, yet that driving force that propels us toward eternal things is unstoppable. In addition, the seal of God's holiness sets us apart for Himself to find our place of origin and our destination –the Kingdom of Heaven!

50

ΠΕΧΕ·ΙC
Said Jesus

ΧΕ	ΕΥ·ϢΑΝ·ΧΟ·ΟC	ΝΗ·ΤΝ	ΧΕ	ΝΤΑ-
this:	If-they-should-speak	to-you(pl)	this-	"Have-

-ΤΕΤΝ·ϢϢΠΕ	ΕΒΟΛ	ΤϢΝ	·ΧΟ·ΟC	ΝΑ·Υ
-you(pl)-come-into-being	out	(of) where?"	Speak	to-them

ΧΕ	ΝΤΑΝ·ΕΙ	ΕΒΟΛ	2Μ·Π·ΟΥΟΕΙΝ	Π·ΜΑ
this-	"We-have-come	out	of-the-light,	the-place

ΕΝΤΑ·Π·ΟΥΟΕΙΝ	·ϢϢΠΕ	Μ·ΜΑΥ	ΕΒΟΛ
which-the-light	came-into-being	there,	outward

2Ι·ΤΟΟΤ·ϥ	ΟΥΑΑΤ·ϥ	Αϥ·Ϣ[2Ε	Ε·ΡΑΤ·ϥ]
by-his-hand	himself;	he-stood	to-his-feet,

[Α]ΥϢ	Αϥ·ΟΥϢ[Ν2]	[ΕΒ]ΟΛ	[2]Ν·ΤΟΥ·2ΙΚϢΝ	ΕΥ·
and	he-appeared	forth	in-their-image."	> If-they-

·ϢΑ·ΧΟ·ΟC	ΝΗ·ΤΝ	ΧΕ	Ν·ΤϢ·ΤΝ	ΠΕ	·ΧΟ·ΟC
-should-speak	to-you(pl)	this-	"You(pl)	are (him)? ",	speak

ΧΕ	ΑΝΟ·Ν	ΝΕϥ·ϢΗΡΕ	ΑΥϢ	ΑΝΟ·Ν	Ν·CϢΤΠ
this-	" We (are)	his-sons,	and	we (are)	the-chosen

Μ·Π·ΕΙϢΤ	ΕΤ·ΟΝ2	ΕΥ·ϢΑΝ·ΧΝΕ·ΘΗΥΤΝ
of-the-father	who-lives."	> If-they-should-ask-yourselves

ΧΕ	ΟΥ	ΠΕ	Π·ΜΑΕΙΝ	Μ·ΠΕΤΝ·ΕΙϢΤ	ΕΤ·2Ν·
this:	"What	is	the-sign	of-your(pl)-father	which-is-in-

·ΘΗΥΤΝ	·ΧΟ·ΟC	ΕΡΟ·ΟΥ	ΧΕ	ΟΥ·ΚΙΜ	ΠΕ	ΜΝ·
-yourselves?",	speak	to-them	this-	"A-movement	it-is,	and-

·ΟΥ·ΑΝΑΠΑΥCΙC
-a-repose."

Jesus said, "If they say to you, 'Where did you come from?', say to them, 'We came from the light, the place where the light came into being on its own accord and established [itself] and became manifest through their image.' If they say to you, 'Is it you?' say, 'We are its children, and we are the elect of the living father.' If they ask you, 'What is the sign of your father in you?', say to them, 'It is movement and repose.' "

We come from Him, this is from His divine essence of life: His Light. He irradiates our spirit with His Light so that we may know Him.

He is our Father from whom we draw our identity to be able to know Him. He chose us before the world was.

His Kingdom is limitless in possibilities and is in constant motion. His voice is constantly speaking; His creation, creating, His heart, loving; His forgiveness, forgiving; His light, radiating. His rest is the promise of His continual movement and rulership. The same dynamic operates in those who belong to him.

51

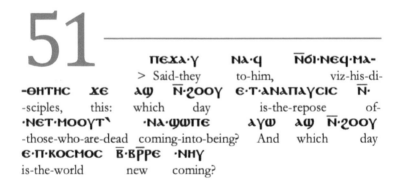

ΠΕΧΑ·Υ	ΝΑ·Ϥ	Ν̅ϬΙ·ΝΕϤ·ΜΑ-
> Said-they	to-him,	viz-his-di-
-ΘΗΤΗC XE	Αϣ Ν̅·2ΟΟΥ	Ε·Τ·ΑΝΑΠΑΥCΙC Ν̅·
-sciples, this:	which day	is-the-repose of-
·ΝΕΤ·ΜΟΟΥΤ`	·ΝΑ·ϣϢΠΕ	ΑΥϢ Αϣ Ν̅·2ΟΟΥ
-those-who-are-dead	coming-into-being?	And which day
Ε·Π·ΚΟCΜΟC	Β̅·Β̅ΡΡΕ ·ΝΗΥ	
is-the-world	new coming?	

His disciples said to him, "When will the repose of the dead come about, and when will the new world come?" He said to them, "What you look forward to has already come, but you do not recognize it."

INTERPRETATION:

The disciples are asking Jesus when the resurrection will come and when the new world will be (the age to come with a better covenant).

Jesus answers, letting them know that it is not a "when" but a "who".

He is the resurrection of the dead. He is the new world. He is the reality of all things, not a theological theory.

52

| | | | ПЄΧΑ·Y |
| | | | Said-they |

NA·q	ÑϬІ·NЄq·МАΘНТНС	ΧЄ	ΧΟΥΤ·АqТЄ
to-him,	viz-his-disciples,	this:	Twenty-four

М·ПРОФНТНС	АY·ϢАΧЄ	2М·П·ІСРАНА`
prophets,	they-spoke	in-Israel,

АYШ	АY·ϢАΧЄ	ТНР·ОY	2РАЇ	Ñ·2НТ·К`	ПЄ`
and	they-spoke,	allofthem,	down	in-you(sg).	Sa-

-ΧΑ·q	NA·Y	ΧЄ	АТЄТÑ·КШ	М·ПЄТ·ОН2	М·ПЄ-
-id-he	to-them	this:	you(pl)-have-left	he-who-lives	in-your-

-ТÑ·ḦТО	ЄВОΛ АYШ	АТЄТÑ·ϢАΧЄ	2А·NЄТ·
-(pl)-presence ( ), and		you(pl)-spoke	about-those-who-are-

·МООYТ`
-dead.

His disciples said to him, "Twenty-four prophets spoke in Israel, and all of them spoke in you." He said to them, "You have omitted the one living in your presence and have spoken (only) of the dead."

INTERPRETATION:

1 Peter 1:10 refers to this passage.

 "Of this salvation the prophets have inquired and searched carefully, who prophesied of the grace that would come to you, searching what, or what manner of time, the Spirit of Christ who was in them was indicating when He testified beforehand the sufferings of Christ and the glories that would follow."

The prophets dwelt inside the Spirit of Christ, from which came forth the annunciation of the knowledge of Jesus, who would come and fulfill every word that came out from Him.

Jesus tells them that He is the living word and stands before them. All other sent prophets of that time had already passed.

53

ΠΕΧΑ·Υ   ΝΑ·Ϥ   ΝϬΙ·ΝΕϤ·ΜΑΘΗΤΗС
Said-they   to-him,   viz-his-disciples,

ΧΕ   Π·СΒΒΕ ·Р·ШФΕλΕΙ Η   Η·ΜΟ·Ν ΠΕΧΑ·Ϥ
this: (Is) circumcision beneficial or (not) to-us? > Said-he

ΝΑ·Υ   ΧΕ   ΝΕϤ·Р·ШФΕλΕΙ ΝΕ·ΠΟΥ·ΕΙШΤ ·ΝΑ·
to-them this: If-he-were-beneficial, their-father (would)-

·ΧΠΟ·ΟΥ ΕΒΟλ 2Ν·ΤΟΥ·ΜΑΑΥ   ΕΥ·СΒΒΗΥ
-beget-them out of-their-mother (already) ()circumcized.

ΑλλΑ Π·СΒΒΕ Η·ΜΕ 2Η·ΠΝΑ ΑϤ·ϬΝ·2ΗΥ
Rather, circumcision true in-spirit, (he)has-found-profit,

ΤΗР·Ϥ
all-of-it.

His disciples said to him, "Is circumcision beneficial or not?" He said to them, "If it were beneficial, their father wouldbeget them already circumcised from their mother. Rather, the true circumcision in spirit has become completely profitable."

INTERPRETATION:

This passage is analogous to

❝ **1 Corinthians 7:19**
"Circumcision is nothing and uncircumcision is nothing, but keeping the commandments of God is what matters."

❝ **Colossians 2:11**
"In Him you were also circumcised with the circumcision made without hands, by putting off the body of the sins of the flesh, by the circumcision of Christ."

54

ⲡⲉϫⲉ·ⲓⲥ	ϫⲉ	ⲍ̄ⲛ·ⲙⲁⲕⲁⲣⲓⲟⲥ	ⲛⲉ	ⲛ·ⲍ̄ⲏ-
Said Jesus	this:	()-blessed-ones	are	the-po-

-ⲕⲉ	ϫⲉ	ⲧⲱ·ⲧ̄ⲛ	ⲧⲉ	ⲧ·ⲙ̄ⲛ̄ⲧⲉⲣⲟ·ⲛ·ⲙ̄·ⲡⲏⲩⲉ`
-or,	for	yours	is	the-kingdom-of(the)heaven(s).

Jesus said, "Blessed are the poor, for yours is the kingdom of heaven."

INTERPRETATION:

It is analogous to

Matthew 5:3

"Blessed are the poor in spirit, for theirs is the kingdom of heaven."

55

	ϫⲉ	ⲡⲉⲧⲁ·ⲙⲉⲥⲧⲉ·ⲡⲉϥ·`·ⲉⲓⲱⲧ`
	this:	Whoever-hates-his- \ -father

ⲁⲛ`	ⲙ̄ⲛ·ⲧⲉϥ·ⲙⲁⲁⲩ	ϥ·ⲛⲁ·ϣ·ⲣ̄·ⲙⲁⲑⲏⲧⲏⲥ	ⲁⲛ
not ,	and-his-mother,	he-can-become-disciple	not

ⲛⲁ·ⲉⲓ`	ⲁⲩⲱ	ⲛ̄ϥ·ⲙⲉⲥⲧⲉ·ⲛⲉϥ·`·ⲥⲛⲏⲩ`	ⲙ̄ⲛ·
to-me,	> and	()()-hates-his- \-brothers	and-

·ⲛⲉϥ·ⲥⲱⲛⲉ	ⲛ̄ϥ·ϥⲉⲓ	ⲙ̄·ⲡⲉϥ·ⲥ·ⲣⲟⲥ	ⲛ̄·ⲧⲁ·ⲍⲉ
-his-sisters,	&()-take	his-cross	in-my-way,

ϥ·ⲛⲁ·ϣⲱⲡⲉ	ⲁⲛ	ⲉϥ·ⲟ	ⲛ̄·ⲁϫⲓⲟⲥ	ⲛⲁ·ⲉⲓ
he-will-come-to-be	not	()being	deserving	to-me.

Jesus said, "Whoever does not hate his father and his mother cannot become a disciple to me. And whoever does not hate his brothers and sisters and take up his cross in my way will not be worthy of me."

The passage is analogous to

Luke 14:26

"If anyone comes to Me and does not hate his father and mother, wife and children, brothers and sisters, yes, and his own life also, he cannot be My disciple."

Being a disciple of Jesus implies being able to leave everything behind to follow Him. He is the priority, and we must be willing to forsake any hindrance from other sources.

56

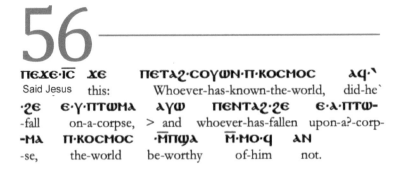

ПЕХЕ·ІC	ХЕ	ПЕТА2·СОΥШΝ·П·КОСМОС	АЧ·ˋ
Said Jesus	this:	Whoever-has-known-the-world,	did-heˋ

·2Є	Є·Υ·ПТШМА	АΥШ	ПЄΝТА2·2Є	Є·А·ПТШ-
-fall	on-a-corpse,	> and	whoever-has-fallen	upon-a?-corp-

-МА	П·КОСМОС	·МПША	М·МО·Ч	АΝ
-se,	the-world	be-worthy	of-him	not.

Jesus said, "Whoever has come to understand the world has found (only) a corpse, and whoever has found a corpse is superior to the world."

The system or the world is disconnected from God as the source of life, and therefore lacks the power to reproduce it. Its substance is death, a corpse. To the degree that we allow Christ and His light and life to radiate within us, we are set free from those ways of death. That corpse is in no way worthy of those in whom the resurrection and life of Christ operate.

57

ΠΕΧΕ·ΙC	ΧΕ	Τ·ΜΝΤΕΡΟ	Μ·Π·ΕΙΩΤ`	ΕC·ΤΝΤΩ
Said Jesus	this:	the-kingdom	of-the-father,	she-compares

Α·Υ·ΡΩΜΕ	ΕΥΝ·ΤΑ·q	Μ·ΜΑΥ	Ν·ΝΟΥ·6ΡΟ6
to-a-man	who-had-he	there	a-seed

[Ε·ΝΑΝΟΥ·]q`	Α·ΠΕq·ΧΑΧΕ	·ΕΙ	Ν·Τ·ΟΥϢΗ`
good() ;	> did-his-enemy	come	in-the-night;

Αq·ϹΙΤΕ	Ν·ΟΥ·ΖΙΖΑΝΙ[ΟΝ	ΕΧ]Ν·ΠΕ·6ΡΟ[6	Ε]-
he-sowed	a-weed	upon-the-seed	which-

-Τ·ΝΑΝΟΥ·q`	ΜΠΕ·Π·ΡΩΜΕ	·ΚΟΟ·Υ	Ε·2ΩΛΕ
-was-good().	> Did-not-the-man	permit-them	to-pullup

Μ·Π·ΖΙΖΑΝΙΟΝ	ΠΕΧΑ·q	ΝΑ·Υ	ΧΕ	ΜΗΠΩϹ
the-weed.	Said-he	to-them	this:	So-that-not

ΝΤΕΤΝ·ΒΩΚ`	ΧΕ	ΕΝΑ·2ΩΛΕ	Μ·Π·ΖΙΖΑΝΙΟ
&-you(pl)-go	for	to-pullup(?)	the-weed

ΝΤΕΤΝ·2ΩΛΕ	Μ·Π·ϹΟΥΟ	ΝΜΜΑ·q`	2Μ·ΦΟ-
&-you(pl)-pullup	the-grain	with-him.	> (for) On-the-da-

-ΟΥ	ΓΑΡ	Μ·Π·Ω2Ϲ	Ν·ΖΙΖΑΝΙΟΝ	·ΝΑ·ΟΥΩΝ2
-y,	(---),	of-the-harvest,	the-weeds	will-appear

ΕΒΟΛ`	ϹΕ·2ΟΛ·ΟΥ	ΝϹΕ·ΡΟΚ2·ΟΥ
forth;	they-pull-them-up	&-()-burn-them.

Jesus said, "The kingdom of the father is like a man who had [good] seed. His enemy came by night and sowed weeds among the good seed. The man did not allow them to pull up the weeds; he said to them, 'I am afraid that you will go intending to pull up the weeds and pull up the wheat along with them.' For on the day of the harvest the weeds will be plainly visible, and they will be pulled up and burned."

INTERPRETATION:

The verse is analogous to

Matthew 13:24-30

"He put forth to them, saying: "The kingdom of heaven is like a man who sowed good seed in his field; but while men slept, his enemy came and sowed tares among the wheat and went his way. But when the grain had sprouted and produced a crop, then the tares also appeared. So the servants of the owner came and said to him, 'Sir, did you not sow good seed in your field? How then does it have tares?' He said to them, 'An enemy has done this.' The servants said to him, 'Do you want us then to go and gather them up?' But he said, 'No, lest while you gather up the tares you also uproot the wheat with them. Let both grow together until the harvest, and at the time of harvest I will say to the reapers, 'First gather together the tares and bind them in bundles to burn them but gather the wheat into my barn.'"

58

				ΠΕΧΕ·ΙC
				Said Jesus

ХЄ	ОУ·МАКАРІОС	ΠЄ	Π·ΡШМЄ	NTА2·2ІСЄ
this:	a-blessed-one	is	the-man	who-is-troubled;

АЧ·2Є	А·Π·ШN2			
he-fell	to(the)Life.			

Jesus said, "Blessed is the man who has suffered and found life."

INTERPRETATION:

Faith is tried by fire, thus making it more valuable than gold.

James 1:2-4

"My brethren, count it all joy when you fall into various trials, knowing that the testing of your faith produces patience. But let patience have its perfect work, that you may be perfect and complete, lacking nothing."

James 5:11

"Indeed, we count them blessed who endure. You have heard of the perseverance of Job and seen the end intended by the Lord—that the Lord is very compassionate and merciful."

Jesus is clear in His words. If the master was persecuted, his disciples could expect the same, "you shall be despised of all men for my name's sake, but he who endures to the end shall be saved."

59

ΠΕΧΕ·Ι͞C	ΧΕ	·ϬѠϢΤ`	Ñ·ϹΑ·ΠΕ-
Said Jesus	this:	Look	after-he-

-Τ·ΟΝ2	2ѠC	ΕΤΕΤÑ·ΟΝ2	2ΙΝΑ	ΧΕ	ΝΕΤÑ·ΜΟΥ
-who-lives	while	you(pl)-are-living,	lest	that	you(pl)-die,

ΑΥѠ	Ñ·ΤΕΤÑ·ϢΙΝΕ	Ε·ΝΑΥ	ΕΡΟ·Ϥ	ΑΥѠ	ΤΕΤΝΑϢ·
and	()you(pl)-seek	to-look	at-him,	and	you(pl)-can-

·ϬΜ·ϬΟΜ	ΑΝ
-find-power	not

Jesus said, "Take heed of the living one while you are alive, lest you die and seek to see him and be unable to do so."

INTERPRETATION:

Jesus relates his kingdom of life to sight, as a spiritual sense to see Him. Before his death and resurrection, he announces to his disciples that they will see him even though the world won't see him anymore. He also expounds how the realm of death (the world) also implies a spiritual numbness and inability to enter his Kingdom of Light, thus linking death with our failure to see him.

Do not take your eyes off Jesus, lest we find death and then want to see him and cannot.

> **Isaiah 55:6-7**
>
> "Seek the Lord while He may be found. Call upon Him while He is near. Let the wicked forsake his way and the unrighteous man his thoughts. Let him return to the Lord, and He will have mercy on him. And to our God, for He will abundantly pardon."

60

ⲉ·ⲚⲀⲨ   Ⲁ·Ⲩ·ⲤⲀⲘⲀⲢⲈⲓⲦⲎⲤ   ⲉϥ·ϥⲓ   Ⲛ·
to-look(?)   at-a-Samaritan   taking   -

·ⲚⲞⲨ·ϨⲓⲉⲓⲂ`   ⲉϥ·ⲂⲎⲔ`   ⲉϨⲞⲨⲚ   ⲉ·ⲦⲞⲨⲆⲀⲓⲀ   ⲠⲈ-
-a-lamb,   __   going   in   to-Judea.   > Sa-

-ⲬⲀ·ϥ`   Ⲛ·ⲚⲈϥ·`·ⲘⲀⲐⲎⲦⲎⲤ   ⲬⲈ   ⲠⲎ   Ⲙ·Ⲡ·ⲔⲰⲦⲈ
-id-he   to-his-   -disciples   this: "That-one (is)   (around)

Ⲙ·ⲠⲈ·ϨⲓⲉⲓⲂ`   ⲠⲈⲬⲀ·Ⲩ   ⲚⲀ·ϥ   ⲬⲈⲔⲀⲀⲤ   ⲉϥ·ⲚⲀ·
the-lamb."   > Said-they   to-him (this)   "Sothat   he-might-

·ⲘⲞⲞⲨⲦ·ϥ`   Ⲛϥ·ⲞⲨⲞⲘ·ϥ`   ⲠⲈⲬⲀ·ϥ   ⲚⲀ·Ⲩ   ϨⲰⲤ   ⲉ-
-kill-him   & -eat-him."   > Said-he   to-them (this) "While   -

-ϥ·ⲞⲚϨ   ϥ·ⲚⲀ·ⲞⲨⲞⲘ·ϥ`   ⲀⲚ   ⲀⲖⲖⲀ   ⲉϥ·ϢⲀ·ⲘⲞ-
-he-is-living,   he-will-eat-him   not;   Rather,   if-he-should-ki-

-ⲞⲨⲦ·ϥ`   Ⲛϥ·ϢⲰⲠⲈ   Ⲛ·ⲞⲨ·ⲠⲦⲰⲘⲀ   ⲠⲈⲬⲀ·Ⲩ
-ll-him   &-he-come-to-be   a-corpse."   > Said-they

ⲬⲈ   Ⲛ·ⲔⲈ·ⲤⲘⲞⲦ`   ϥ·ⲚⲀϢ·Ⲁ·Ⲥ   ⲀⲚ   ⲠⲈⲬⲀ·ϥ   ⲚⲀ·Ⲩ
this: "Another-way   he-can-do   not."   > Said-he   to-them

ⲬⲈ   Ⲛ·ⲦⲰ·ⲦⲚ   ϨⲰⲦ·`·ⲦⲎⲨⲦⲚ   ·ϢⲓⲚⲈ   ⲚⲤⲀ·ⲞⲨ·
this: "You(pl)   also-\-yourselves   seek   after-a-

·ⲦⲞⲠⲞⲤ   ⲚⲎ·ⲦⲚ   ⲉϨⲞⲨⲚ   ⲉ·Ⲩ·ⲀⲚⲀⲠⲀⲨⲤⲓⲤ
-place   for-you(rselves)   in   a-repose,

ⲬⲈⲔⲀⲀⲤ   ⲚⲚⲈⲦⲚ·ϢⲰⲠⲈ   Ⲙ·ⲠⲦⲰⲘⲀ   ⲚⲤⲈ·
sothat   not-you(pl)-come-to-be   corpses   &-they-

·ⲞⲨⲰⲘ·`·ⲦⲎⲨⲦⲚ
-eat-\   -yourselves."

<They saw> a Samaritan carrying a lamb on his way to Judea. He said to his disciples, "That man is

round about the lamb." They said to him, "So that he may kill it and eat it." He said to them, "While it is alive, he will not eat it, but only when he has killed it and it has become a corpse." They said to him, "He cannot do so otherwise." He said to them, "You too, look for a place for yourselves within repose, lest you become a corpse and be eaten."

INTERPRETATION:

The term corpse describes the system's state of death throughout the text. Life does not belong to the system, nor can it contain it. Rather the system seeks to devour life.

Those absorbed by the system are in the same state of death. Jesus speaks to us about entering the Father's rest as the solution.

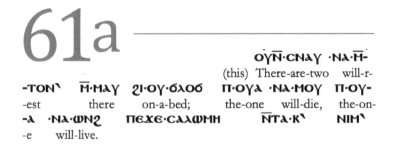

Jesus said, "Two will rest on a bed: the one will die, and the other will live."

INTERPRETATION:

This verse is analogous to

Luke 17:34

"I tell you, on that night there will be two men in one bed: the one will be taken and the other will be left."

61b

ΠΕΧΕ·ϹΑⲖⲰⲘⲎ				ⲚⲦⲀ·Ⲕ`		ⲚⲒⲘ`
Said-Salome			(this)	"You(sg)	(are)	who,

Π·ⲢⲰⲘⲈ	ⲌⲰϹ	ⲈⲂⲞⲖ	ⲌⲚ·ⲞⲨⲀ	ⲀⲔ·ⲦⲈⲖⲞ	ⲈⲬⲘ·
man?	As-if	out	of-one,	did-you(sg)-climb	onto-

·ⲠⲀ·ϬⲖⲞϬ	ⲀⲨⲰ	ⲀⲔ·`·ⲞⲨⲰⲘ	ⲈⲂⲞⲖ	ⲌⲚ·ⲦⲀ·
-my-bed,	and	did-you(sg)- -eat	off	of-my-

·ⲦⲢⲀⲠⲈⲌⲀ	ΠΕΧΕ·ⲒⲤ	ⲚⲀ·Ϲ	ⲬⲈ	ⲀⲚⲞ·Ⲕ`	ΠⲈ
-table."	Said Jesus	to-her	this:	" I	am

ΠⲈⲦ·ϢⲞⲞΠ`	ⲈⲂⲞⲖ	ⲌⲘ·ΠⲈⲦ·`·ϢⲎϢ	ⲀⲨ·Ⲧ
he-who-exists	out	of-he-who-\-is-equal;	they-gave

ⲚⲀ·ⲈⲒ	ⲈⲂⲞⲖ	ⲌⲚ·ⲚⲀ·ΠⲀ·ⲈⲒⲰⲦ`	ⲀⲚⲞ·Ⲕ`	ⲦⲈⲔ·`
to-me	out	of-that-of-my-father."	> I (am)	your(sg)-

·ⲘⲀⲐⲎⲦⲎϹ	ⲈⲦⲂⲈ·ΠⲀⲈⲒ	Ⲧ·ⲬⲰ	Ⲙ·ⲘⲞ·Ϲ	ⲬⲈ
-disciple.	Because-of-this,	I-speak	( )	this:

ⲌⲞⲦⲀⲚ	ⲈϤ·ϢⲀ·ϢⲰΠⲈ	ⲈϤ·ϢⲎϤ`	Ϥ·ⲚⲀ·ⲘⲞⲨⲌ
when	he-should-come-to-be	()destroyed,	he-will-be-full

ⲞⲨⲞⲈⲒⲚ	ⲌⲞⲦⲀⲚ	ⲆⲈ	ⲈϤ·ϢⲀⲚ·ϢⲰΠⲈ	ⲈϤ·
(of?)light;	when,	hwvr,	he-should-come-to-be	he-

·ΠⲎϢ	Ϥ·ⲚⲀ·ⲘⲞⲨⲌ	Ⲛ·ⲔⲀⲔⲈ
-divided,	he-will-be-full	of-darkness.

Salome says: "Who art thou, man; from whom hast thou <come forth,> that thou shouldst lie on my couch and eat at my table?" Jesus says to her: "I am he who has been brought into being by Him who is equal <to me:> I have been given what belongs to my Father!"—"I am thy disciple!"

Because of that, I say this: When <a person> finds himself solitary, he will be full of light; but when he finds himself divided, he will be full of darkness.

INTERPRETATION:

The topics of this verse are division and unity. One understands the passage in a Coptic context in which someone of importance or a great friend reclined on a couch or kneeler, typical of where the meal was eaten. Salome - whom we do not know who she was - asks Jesus who he is that so confidently sits at his table (some translations say bed instead of couch, yet the correct translation is a couch or a lounger).

Jesus, who picks up on Salome's way of separating herself from him by treating him almost as an intruder, answers her about the essence of Unity. He is one, Elohim.

This verse speaks to us of oneness, of becoming one with Him, and only then will we be filled with the light of His resurrection. While we remain separated, we are in a state of death.

62

ⲡⲉⲝⲉ·ⲓ̅ⲥ̅ ⲝⲉ ⲉⲓ·
Said Jesus this: I-

·ⲝⲱ ⲛ̅·ⲛⲁ·ⲙⲩⲥⲧⲏⲣⲓⲟⲛ ⲛ̅·ⲛ[ⲉⲧ·ⲙ̅ⲡ·ϣ·ⲁ ⲛ̅·]
-speak of-my-mysteries to-those-worthy of-

[·ⲛⲁ·ⲙ]ⲩⲥⲧⲏⲣⲓⲟⲛ ⲡⲉ|ⲧ|ⲉ·ⲧⲉⲕ·ᵛ·ⲟⲩⲛⲁⲙ ·ⲛⲁ·ⲁ·ϥ
my-mysteries. > That-which-your(sg)-\ -right will-do(),

ⲙ̅ⲛ̅ⲧⲣⲉ·ⲧⲉⲕ·ⳉⲃⲟⲩⲣᵛ ·ⲉⲓⲙⲉ ⲝⲉ ⲉⲥ·ⲣ·ⲟⲩ
let-not-your(sg)-left realize that she-is-what.

Jesus said, "It is to those [who are worthy of my] mysteries that I tell my mysteries. Do not let your (sg.) left hand know what your (sg.) right hand is doing."

INTERPRETATION:

In Matthew 6, we find the same words regarding almsgiving. He knows who the good steward is, worthy to receive His mysteries.

Some of the revelations He gives us are just for us, not for the whole world, and others are for the body. However, we must refrain from boasting about what we receive, which is holy and precious to Him.

Matthew 6:3

"But when you do a charitable deed, do not let your left hand know what your right hand is doing."

63

ⲡⲉⲭⲉ·ⲓⲥ
Said Jesus

ⲭⲉ ⲛⲉⲩⲛ·ⲟⲩ·ⲣⲱⲙⲉ ⲙ̄·ⲡⲗⲟⲩⲥⲓⲟⲥ ⲉⲩⲛ̄·ⲧⲁ·ϥ ⲙ̄·
this: There-was-a-man of-wealth who-had-he -

·ⲙⲁⲩ ⲛ̄·ϩⲁϩ ⲛ̄·ⲭⲣⲏⲙⲁ ⲡⲉⲭⲁ·ϥ ⲭⲉ ϯ·ⲛⲁ·ⲣ̄·ⲭⲣⲱ ⲛ̄·
-there many riches. > Said-he this: "I-will-make-use of-

·ⲛⲁ·ⲭⲣⲏⲙⲁ ⲭⲉⲕⲁⲁⲥ ⲉ·ⲉⲓ·ⲛⲁ·ⲭⲟ ⲛ̄ⲧⲁ·ⲱⲥϩ
-my-riches, sothat I-might-sow, &()reap,

ⲛ̄ⲧⲁ·ⲧⲱϭⲉ ⲛ̄ⲧⲁ·ⲙⲟⲩϩ ⲛ̄·ⲛⲁ·ⲉϩⲱⲣ ⲛ̄·ⲕⲁⲣ`
&()plant, &()fill my-treasurehouse with-fru`

·ⲡⲟⲥ ϣⲓⲛⲁ ⲭⲉ ⲛ̄·ⲓ·ⲣ̄·ϭⲣⲱϩ ⲗ̄·ⲗⲁⲁⲩ ⲛⲁⲉⲓ ⲛⲉ
-it, so that I-not-need anything." > These were

ⲛⲉϥ·ⲙⲉⲉⲩⲉ ⲉⲣⲟ·ⲟⲩ ϩⲙ̄·ⲡⲉϥ·ϩⲏⲧ` ⲁⲩⲱ ϩⲛ̄·
his-thoughts about-them in-his-mind; and in-

·ⲧ·ⲟⲩϣⲏ ⲉⲧ·ⲙ̄·ⲙⲁⲩ ⲁϥ·ⲙⲟⲩ ⲡⲉⲧ·ⲉⲩⲙ̄·ⲙⲁⲭⲉ
-the-night which-was-there, he-died. > He-who-has-ear(sic)

ⲙ̄·ⲙⲟ·ϥ` ⲙⲁⲣⲉϥ·`·ⲥⲱⲧⲙ̄
of-him let-him- \ -listen.

Jesus said, "There was a rich man who had much money. He said, 'I shall put my money to use so that I may sow, reap, plant, and fill my storehouse with produce, with the result that I shall lack nothing.' Such were his intentions, but that same night he died. Let him who has ears hear."

INTERPRETATION:

The verse is analogous to

Luke 12:15-21

"And He said to them, 'Take heed and beware of covetousness, for one's life does not consist in the abundance of

the things he possesses.' Then He spoke a parable to them, saying: 'The ground of a certain rich man yielded plentifully.' And he thought within himself, saying, 'What shall I do, since I have no room to store my crops?' So, he said, 'I will do this: I will pull down my barns and build greater, and there I will store all my crops and my goods. And I will say to my soul, 'Soul, you have many goods laid up for many years; take your ease; eat, drink, and be merry.'" But God said to him, 'Fool! This night your soul will be required of you, then whose will those things be which you have provided?' So is he who lays up treasure for himself and is not rich toward God."

He urges us not to waste time focused on material, fleshy, or worldly things. Instead, we must focus on the Spirit who gives us life.

64a

ΠΕΧΕ·ΙC ΧΕ ΟΥ·ΡѠ-
Said Jesus this: a-ma-

-ΜΕ ΝΕΥΝ·ΤΑ·Ϥ·ϨΝ·ѠΜΜΟ ΑΥѠ ΝΤΑΡΕϤ·CΟΒ-
-n was-having-he-some-visitors, and when-he-had-prepar-

-ΤΕ Μ·Π·ΔΙΠΝΟΝ ΑϤ·ΧΟΟΥ Μ·ΠΕϤ·ϨΜϨΑΛ ѠΙ-
-ed the-dinner, he-sent his-servant, so-

-ΝΑ ΕϤ·ΝΑ·ΤѠϨΜ Ν·Ν·ѠΜΜΟΕΙ ΑϤ·ΒѠΚ` Μ·
-that he-might-call the-visitors. > Did-he-go to-

·Π·ѠΟΡΠ` ΠΕΧΑ·Ϥ ΝΑ·Ϥ` ΧΕ ΠΑ·ΧΟΕΙC ·ΤѠϨΜ
-the-first. > Said-he to-him this: "My-Lord calls

Μ·ΜΟ·Κ` ΠΕΧΑ·Ϥ ΧΕ ΟΥΝ·ΤΑ·ΕΙ·ϨΝ·ϨΟΜΤ`
you(sg)." Said-he this: "Have-I-some-money

Α·ϨΕΝ·ΕΜΠΟΡΟC CΕ·ΝΝΗΥ ѠΑΡΟ·ΕΙ Ε·ΡΟΥϨΕ
for-some-traders; they-are-coming upto-me (at?)evening;

Ϯ·ΝΑ·ΒѠΚ` ΝΤΑ·ΟΥΕϨ·CΑϨΝΕ ΝΑ·Υ Ϯ·Ρ·ΠΑΡΑΙ-
I-will-go &()-place-orders to-them; I-beg-

-ΤΕΙ Μ·Π·ΔΙΠΝΟΝ ΑϤ·ΒѠΚ` ѠΑ·ΚΕ·ΟΥΑ ΠΕ-
-off the-dinner." > Did-he-go upto-another-one. Sa-

-ΧΑ·Ϥ ΝΑ·Ϥ` ΧΕ Α·ΠΑ·ΧΟΕΙC ·ΤѠϨΜ Μ·ΜΟ·Κ`
-id-he to-him this: "Did-my-Lord call you(sg)."

ΠΕΧΑ·Ϥ ΝΑ·Ϥ ΧΕ ΑΕΙ·ΤΟΟΥ ΟΥ·ΗΕΙ ΑΥѠ CΕ·
Said-he to-him this: "I-have-bought a-house, and they-

·Ρ·ΑΙΤΕΙ Μ·ΜΟ·ΕΙ Ν·ΟΥ·ϨΗΜΕΡΑ Ϯ·ΝΑ·CΡϤΕ Α
-require of-me a-days-time; I-will-be-at-rest not

ΑϤ·ΕΙ ѠΑ·ΚΕ·ΟΥΑ ΠΕΧΑ·Ϥ ΝΑ·Ϥ` ΧΕ ΠΑ·ΧΟ-
He-came upto-another-one. Said-he to-him this: "My-Lo-

-ΕΙC ·ΤѠϨΜ Μ·ΜΟ·Κ` ΠΕΧΑ·Ϥ ΝΑ·Ϥ ΧΕ ΠΑ·ѠΒΗΡ
-rd calls you(sg)." > Said-he to-him this: "My-friend

·ΝΑ·P·ϢΕλΕΕΤ   ΑΥⲰ   ΑΝΟ·Κˋ   ΕΤ·ΝΑ·P·ΔΙΠΝΟΝ
-will-be-married   and   I,   who-will-make-dinner,

†·ΝΑϢ·Ι   ΑΝ   †·P·ΠΑΡΑΙΤΕΙ   Μ̄·Π·ΔΙΠΝΟΝˋ   ΑϤˋ
I-can-come not;   I-beg-off   of-the-dinner." > Did-he-

·ΒⲰΚˋ   ϢΑ·ΚΕ·ΟΥΑ   ΠΕΧΑ·Ϥ   ΝΑ·Ϥ   ΧΕ   ΠΑ·ΧΟΕΙΣ
-go   upto-another-one. Said-he   to-him   this: " My-Lord

·ΤⲰ2Μ   Μ̄·ΜΟ·Κˋ   ΠΕΧΑ·Ϥ   ΝΑ·Ϥˋ   ΧΕ   ΑΕΙ·ΤΟΟΥ   Ν̄·
-calls   you(sg)."   > Said-he   to-him   this: "I-have-bought -

·ΟΥ·ΚⲰΜΗ   Ε·ΕΙ·ΒΗΚˋ   Α·ΧΙ   Ν̄·ϢⲰΜ   †·ΝΑϢ·Ι
-a-farm;   I-am-going   to-take   the-taxes.   I-can-come

ΑΝ   †·P·ΠΑΡΑΙΤΕΙ   ΑϤ·ΕΙ   Ν̄ϬΙ·Π·2Μ2Αλ   ΑϤ·ΧΟ·
not;   I-beg-off."   > He-came,   viz-the-servant,   he-spo-

·ΟΣ   Α·ΠΕϤ·ΧΟΕΙΣ   ΧΕ   ΝΕΝΤΑΚ·ˋ·ΤΑ2Μ·ΟΥ   Α·
-ke   to-his-Lord   this-   "Those-you(sg)-did-\-call-them   to-

·Π·ΔΙΠΝΟΝ   ΑΥ·ΠΑΡΑΙΤΕΙ   ΠΕΧΕ·Π·ΧΟΕΙΣ   Μ̄·
-the-dinner,   they-have-begged-off."   > Said-the-Lord   to-

·ΠΕϤ·2Μ2Αλ   ΧΕ   ·ΒⲰΚˋ   Ε·Π·ΣΑ·Ν·ΒΟλ   Α·Ν·2ΙΟ-
-his-servant   this: " Go   to-the-side-outer,   to-the-ro-

-ΟΥΕ   ΝΕΤ·Κ·ΝΑ·2Ε   ΕΡΟ·ΟΥ   ·ΕΝΙ·ΟΥ   ΧΕΚΑΑΣ
-ads; those-who-you(sg)-will-fall   on-them,   bring-them,   sothat

ΕΥ·ΝΑ·P·ΔΙΠΝΕΙ
they-may-dine."

Jesus said, "A man had received visitors. And when he had prepared the dinner, he sent his servant to invite the guests. He went to the first one and said to him, 'My master invites you.' He said, 'I have claims against some merchants. They are coming to me this evening. I must go and give them my orders. I ask to be excused from the dinner.' He went to another and said to him, 'My master has invited you.' He said to him, 'I have just bought a house and am required for the day. I shall not have any spare time.' He went to another and said to him, 'My master invites you.' He said to him, 'My friend is going to get married, and I am to prepare the banquet. I shall not be able to come. I ask to be excused from the dinner.' He went to another and said to him, 'My master invites you.' He said to him, 'I have just bought a farm, and I am on my way to collect the rent. I shall not be able to come. I ask to be excused.' The servant returned and said to his master, 'Those whom you invited to the dinner have asked to be excused.' The master said to his servant, 'Go outside to the streets and bring back those whom you happen to meet, so that they may dine.'

INTERPRETATION:

This saying is analogous to **Matthew 22:1-9**

 "And Jesus answered and spoke to them again by parables and said: 'The kingdom of heaven is like a certain king who arranged a marriage for his son and sent out his servants to call those who were invited to the wedding; and they were not willing to come. Again, he sent out other servants, saying, 'Tell those who are invited, 'See, I have prepared my dinner; my oxen and fatted cattle are killed, and all things are ready. Come to the wedding.' But they made light of it and went their ways, one to his own farm, another to his business. And the rest seized his servants, treated them spitefully, and killed them. But when the king heard about it, he was furious. And he sent out his armies, destroyed those murderers, and burned up their city. Then he said to his servants, 'The wedding is ready, but those who were invited were not worthy. Therefore, go into the highways, and as many as you find, invite to the wedding.'"

64b

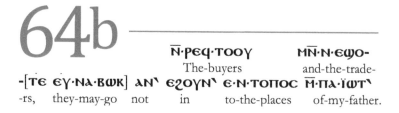

Ν·ΡΕϤ·ΤΟΟΥ   ΜΝ·Ν·ΕϢΟ-
The-buyers   and-the-trade-

-[ΤΕ ΕΥ·ΝΑ·ΒΩΚ] ΑΝ˅ ΕϨΟΥΝ˅ Ε·Ν·ΤΟΠΟϹ Μ·ΠΑ·ΪΩΤ˅
-rs,   they-may-go   not   in   to-the-places   of-my-father.

Businessmen and merchants [will] not enter the places of my father."

INTERPRETATION:

The verse does not refer to a merchant being denied salvation. Of course, he can. Jesus is referring to the way of looking at this world's goods and the unrighteous way of selling them. The commercial system can be very corrupt and filled with greed.

Finances have the power to possess the heart of men and to make them slaves. Selling can be righteous if a person's heart is focused on God and doing the right thing.

On the other hand, commerce is an enterprise that demands a person's entire involvement, so much that it absorbs him entirely by the amount of demands and details it requires.

The 'Father's places' are glorious dimensions one may enter by resting in our inner being and engaging in contemplative prayer and adoration through the Spirit.

These things require time and dedication, and a person too entangled in the business world will hardly have time for this type of consecration.

The Apostle Paul refers to it when he speaks to Timothy about his service to the Lord.

> **2 Timothy 2:4**
>
> "No one engaged in warfare entangles himself with the affairs of this life, that he may please Him who enlisted him as a soldier."

65

ⲡⲉϫⲁ·ϥ ϫⲉ ⲟⲩ·ⲣⲱⲙⲉ ⲛ̄·ⲭⲣⲏ[ⲥⲧⲟ]ⲥ ⲛⲉⲩⲛ̄·[·ⲧⲁ·ϥ]
Said-he this: A-man of-justice was-having()
ⲛ̄·ⲟⲩ·ⲙⲁ ⲛ̄·ⲉⲗⲟⲟⲗⲉ ⲁϥ·ⲧⲁⲁ·ϥ ⲛ̄·[ϩ]ⲛ̄·ⲟⲩⲟⲉⲓⲉ
a-place of-grapes; he-gave-him to-some-tenants
ϣⲓⲛⲁ ⲉⲩ·ⲛⲁ·ⲣ̄·ϩⲱⲃ` ⲉⲣⲟ·ϥ` ⲛ̄ϥ·ϫⲓ [ⲙ̄·]ⲡⲉϥ·ⲕⲁⲣ`
so they-might-do-work on-him, &-he-take his-fru\
-ⲡⲟⲥ ⲛ̄·ⲧⲟⲟⲧ·ⲟⲩ ⲁϥ·ϫⲟⲟⲩ ⲙ̄·ⲡⲉϥ·ϩⲙ̄ϩⲁⲗ ϫⲉ-
-it from-their-hand. > He-sent his-servant, so
-ⲕⲁⲁⲥ ⲉ·ⲛ·ⲟⲩⲟⲉⲓⲉ ·ⲛⲁ·ϯ ⲛⲁ·ϥ` ⲙ̄·ⲡ·ⲕⲁⲣⲡⲟⲥ ⲙ̄·
-that the-tenants might-give to-him the-fruit of
·ⲡ·ⲙⲁ ⲛ̄·ⲉⲗⲟⲟⲗⲉ ⲁⲩ·ⲉⲙⲁϩⲧⲉ ⲙ̄·ⲡⲉϥ·ϩⲙ̄ϩⲁⲗ
-the-place of-grapes. > They-grabbed his-servant;
ⲁⲩ·ϩⲓⲟⲩⲉ ⲉⲣⲟ·ϥ` ⲛⲉ·ⲕⲉ·ⲕⲟⲩⲉⲓ ⲡⲉ ⲛ̄ⲥⲉ·ⲙⲟⲟⲩⲧ·ϥ`
they-beat him; had-another-little-bit been, &they-kill-him.
ⲁ·ⲡ·ϩⲙ̄ϩⲁⲗ ·ⲃⲱⲕ` ⲁϥ·ϫⲟ·ⲟⲥ ⲉ·ⲡⲉϥ·ϫⲟⲉⲓⲥ ⲡⲉ-
Did-the-servant go; he-spoke to-his-Lord. > Sa-
-ϫⲉ·ⲡⲉϥ·ϫⲟⲉⲓⲥ ϫⲉ ⲙⲉϣⲁⲕ` ⲙ̄ⲡⲉϥ·`·ⲥⲟⲩⲱ-
-id-his-Lord this: "Perhaps did-not-he(!)\-know-
-ⲛ·ⲟⲩ ⲁϥ·ϫⲟⲟⲩ ⲛ̄·ⲕⲉ·ϩⲙ̄ϩⲁⲗ ⲁ·ⲛ·ⲟⲩⲟⲉⲓⲉ ·ϩⲓ-
-them." > He-sent another-servant; did-the-tenants be-
-ⲟⲩⲉ ⲉ·ⲡ·ⲕⲉ·ⲟⲩⲁ ⲧⲟⲧⲉ ⲁ·ⲡ·ϫⲟⲉⲓⲥ ·ϫⲟⲟⲩ ⲙ̄·
-at the-other-one. > Then did-the-Lord send -
·ⲡⲉϥ·ϣⲏⲣⲉ ⲡⲉϫⲁ·ϥ` ϫⲉ ⲙⲉϣⲁⲕ` ⲥⲉ·ⲛⲁ·ϣⲓⲡⲉ
-his-son. Said-he this: "Perhaps they-will-be-ashamed
ϩⲏⲧ·ϥ` ⲙ̄·ⲡⲁ·ϣⲏⲣⲉ ⲁ·ⲛ·`·ⲟⲩⲟⲉⲓⲉ ⲉⲧ·ⲙ̄·ⲙⲁⲩ ⲉⲡⲉⲓ
before-him, my-son." > Did-the\tenants who-were-there, because
ⲥⲉ·ⲥⲟⲟⲩⲛ ϫⲉ ⲛ̄·ⲧⲟ·ϥ ⲡⲉ ⲡⲉ·ⲕⲗⲏⲣⲟⲛⲟⲙⲟⲥ
they-know that he is the-heir
ⲙ̄·ⲡ·ⲙⲁ ⲛ̄·ⲉⲗⲟⲟⲗⲉ ⲁⲩ·ϭⲟⲡ·ϥ` ⲁⲩ·ⲙⲟⲟⲩⲧ·ϥ`
of-the-place of-grapes, they-seized-him; they-killed-him.
ⲡⲉⲧ·ⲉⲩⲙ̄·ⲙⲁⲁϫⲉ ⲙ̄·ⲙⲟ·ϥ` ⲙⲁⲣⲉϥ·`·ⲥⲱⲧⲙ̄
He-who-has-ear of-him, let-him- \ -listen.

He said, "There was a good man who owned a vineyard. He leased it to tenant farmers so that they might work it and he might collect the produce from them. He sent his servant so that the tenants might give him the produce of the vineyard. They seized his servant and beat him, all but killing him. The servant went back and told his master. The master said, 'Perhaps he did not recognize them.' He sent another servant. The tenants beat this one as well. Then the owner sent his son and said, 'Perhaps they will show respect to my son.' Because the tenants knew that it was he who was the heir to the vineyard, they seized him and killed him. Let him who has ears hear."

INTERPRETATION:

This verse is analogous to

 Matthew 21:33-41
"Hear another parable: There was a certain landowner, who planted a vineyard and set a hedge around it, dug a winepress in it and built a tower. And he leased it to vinedressers and went into a far country. Now when the vintage time drew near, he sent his servants to the vinedressers, that they might receive its fruit. And the vinedressers took his servants, beat one, killed one, and stoned another. Again, he sent other servants, more than the first, and they did likewise to them. Then last of all, he sent his son to them, saying, 'They will respect my son.' But when the vinedressers saw the son, they said among themselves,

'This is the heir. Come, let us kill him and seize his inheritance.' So, they took him, cast him out of the vineyard, and killed him. 'Therefore, when the owner of the vineyard comes, what will he do to those vinedressers?' They said to Him, 'He will destroy those wicked men miserably, and lease his vineyard to other vinedressers who will render to him the fruits in their seasons.' Jesus said to them, 'Have you never read in the Scriptures: 'The stone which the builders rejected has become the chief cornerstone. This was the Lord's doing, and it is marvelous in our eyes? Therefore, I say to you, the kingdom of God will be taken from you and given to a nation bearing the fruits of it. And whoever falls on this stone will be broken; but on whomever it falls, it will grind him to powder.' Now when the chief priests and Pharisees heard His parables, they perceived that He was speaking of them. But when they sought to lay hands on Him, they feared the multitudes, because they took Him for a prophet."

In this parable, Jesus refers to the priesthood of the old covenant. However, the priesthood was corrupted, thus choosing not to listen to the prophets, the voice of God, and went so far as to kill the Son of God.

Greed and selfishness lead the soul of men to prioritize ego, drawing away from the righteousness of God (faith). These men knew that by killing the heir, they could steal the land. We must be watchful not to have them in us, lest they take away the extraordinary inheritance the Son purchased for us with his own life.

66

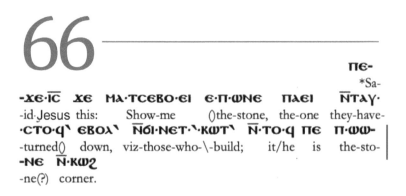

ΠЄ-
*Sa-

-ХЄ·ІС ХЄ МА·ТСЄΒО·ЄІ Є·Π·ШΝЄ ΠΑЄІ ΝΤΑΥ·
-id·Jesus this: Show-me ()the-stone, the-one they-have-
·СΤО·Ϥˋ ЄΒОΛˋ ΝόΙ·ΝЄΤ·ˋ·ΚШΤˋ Ν·ΤО·Ϥ ΠЄ Π·ШШ-
-turned() down, viz-those-who-\-build; it/he is the-sto-
-ΝЄ Ν·ΚШ2
-ne(?) corner.

Jesus said, "Show me the stone which the builders have rejected. That one is the cornerstone."

INTERPRETATION:

This passage is analogous to

 Psalms 118:22
"The stone which the builders rejected has become the chief cornerstone."

Each of us, being a god –lowercase 'g'– builds our limited world. Our ego does not know how to stay still and always wants more and more. The more deeds, the more pride.

During Jesus' time, the religious system led by the Pharisees focused on human titles and the splendor of the earthly temple. By exalting themselves, these builders rejected Jesus, the true cornerstone.

We can extend this saying to

> **Matthew 21:44**
> "' And whoever falls on this stone will be broken; but on whomever it falls, it will grind him to powder.' Now when the chief priests and Pharisees heard His parables, they perceived that He was speaking of them. But when they sought to lay hands on Him, they feared the multitudes, because they took Him for a prophet."

67

ΠⲈⲬⲈ·ⲒⲤ	ⲬⲈ	ΠⲈⲦ·ⲤⲞⲞⲨⲚ	Ⲙ·Π·ⲦⲎⲢ·ϥ
Said Jesus	this:	He-who-knows	the-all-of-it,

Ⲉϥ·Ⲣ̄·ϬⲢⲰ2	ⲞⲨⲀⲀ·ϥ	·Ⲣ̄·ϬⲢⲰ2	Ⲙ·Π·ⲘⲀ	ⲦⲎⲢ·ϥ`
if-he-needs	himself,	needs	the-place,	all-of-it.

Jesus said, "If one who knows the all still feels a personal deficiency, he is completely deficient."

INTERPRETATION:

Two things are addressed here: first, the knowledge of everything, and then, the knowledge of oneself.

The knowledge of everything consists of being fed by the tree of the knowledge of good and evil, which always leads to death. It is our ego that craves this knowledge to exalt itself.

On the other hand, knowing oneself consists of knowing that we are sons of God. It's identity in the Father in which lies true strength. Without knowing ourselves and our origin, the knowledge of this world will only lead to death.

> **Ephesians 1:3-4**
> "Blessed be the God and Father of our Lord Jesus Christ, who has blessed us with every spiritual blessing in the heavenly places in Christ, just as He chose us in Him before the foundation of the world, that we should be holy and without blame before Him in love."

68

ⲡⲉϫⲉ·ⲓ̅ⲥ̅ ϫⲉ ⲛ̅·ⲧⲱ·ⲧⲛ̅ ϩⲙ̅·ⲙⲁⲕⲁⲣⲓⲟⲥ ϩⲟⲧⲁ
Said Jesus this: You(pl) (are) ( )-blessed-ones when
ⲉⲩ·ϣⲁⲛ·ⲙⲉⲥⲧⲉ·ⲑⲩⲧⲛ̅ ⲛ̅ⲥⲉ·ⲡ̅·ⲇⲓⲱⲕⲉ ⲙ̅·
they-should-hate-yourselves &-( )-persecute -
·ⲙⲱ·ⲧⲛ̅ ⲁⲩⲱ ⲥⲉ·ⲛⲁ·ϩⲉ ⲁⲛ ⲉ·ⲧⲟⲡⲟⲥ ϩⲙ̅·ⲡ·ⲙⲁ
-you(pl), > and they-will-fall not upon-anywhere in-the-place
ⲉⲛⲧⲁⲩ·ⲇⲓⲱⲕⲉ ⲙ̅·ⲙⲱ·ⲧⲛ̅ ϩⲣⲁⲓ̈ ⲛ̅·ϩⲏⲧ·ϥ`
where-they-persecuted you(pl) down in-him.

Jesus said, "Blessed are you when you are hated and persecuted. Wherever you have been persecuted they will find no place."

INTERPRETATION:

The first part of this verse mirrors the beatitude found in

Matthew 5: 10-11

> "Blessed are those who are persecuted for righteousness' sake,

> For theirs is the kingdom of heaven. Blessed are you when they revile and persecute you and say all kinds of evil against you falsely for My sake."

The second part, "Wherever you have been persecuted, they will find no place," refers to the reward of the beatitude: not belonging to this world's system, the place which persecutes and devours, and the righteousness that comes from Heaven.

It is also analogous to

John 15:18-19

"If the world hates you, you know that it hated Me before it hated you. If you were of the world, the world would love its own. Yet because you are not of the world, but I chose you out of the world, therefore the world hates you."

69a

ΠⲈ-
*Sa-

-ⲭⲉ·ⲓ̅ⲥ̅ <>	ⲉ̅ⲙ·ⲙⲁⲕⲁⲣⲓⲟⲥ	ⲛⲉ	ⲛⲁⲉⲓ	ⲛ̅ⲧⲁⲩ·ⲇⲓⲱⲕⲉ
-id Jesus (this)	( )-blessed-ones	are	these	they-have-persecuted
ⲙ̅·ⲙⲟ·ⲟⲩ	ⲉ̅ⲣⲁ̈ⲓ	ⲉ̅ⲙ·ⲡⲟⲩ·ⲉ̅ⲏⲧ`		ⲛⲉⲧ·ⲙ̅·ⲙⲁⲩ`
them	down	in-their-mind;		those-who-are-there,
ⲛⲉⲛⲧⲁⲉ·ⲥⲟⲩⲱⲛ·ⲡ·ⲉⲓⲱⲧ`			ⲉ̅ⲛ·ⲟⲩ·ⲙⲉ	
they-have-known-the-father			(truly).	

Jesus said, "Blessed are they who have been persecuted within themselves. It is they who have truly come to know the father.

INTERPRETATION:

It is analogous to

Luke 12:34

"For where your treasure is, there your heart will be also."

The Father's knowledge and closely guarded secrets, which He reveals to those who genuinely love Him, oppose our natural heart. This triggers internal tension because our unrenewed thoughts and feelings fight the living God.

When the knowledge of the Spirit strives to undo our reasoning, culture, and internal structures, it is a sign that life is manifesting within us and is a great beatitude.

69b

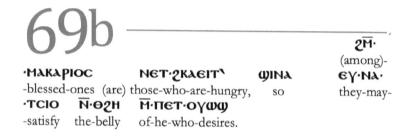

			ϨⲘ·
			(among)-
·ⲘⲀⲔⲀⲢⲒⲞⲤ	ⲚⲈⲦ·ϨⲔⲀⲈⲒⲦ`	ϢⲒⲚⲀ	ⲈⲨ·ⲚⲀ·
-blessed-ones (are)	those-who-are-hungry,	so	they-may-
·ⲦⲤⲒⲞ	Ⲛ·ⲈϨⲎ	Ⲙ·ⲠⲈⲦ·ⲞⲨⲰϢ	
-satisfy	the-belly	of-he-who-desires.	

Blessed are the hungry, for the belly of him who desires will be filled."

INTERPRETATION:

It is analogous to

Matthew 5:6
"Blessed are those who hunger and thirst for righteousness, for they shall be filled."

It speaks about spiritual hunger and thirst. God always seeks a hungry and thirsty heart for Him, and it is unto those to whom God reveals and manifests Himself.

70

ΠΕΧΕ·ΙΣ <> 2Ο-
Said Jesus (this) Wh-

-ΤΑΝ	ΕΤΕΤΝ·ϢΑ·ΧΠΕ·ΠΗ	2Ν·ΤΗΥΤΝ	ΠΑΪ
-en	you(pl)-should-beget-that-one	in-yourselves,	the-one
ΕΤ·ΕΥΝ·ΤΗ·ΤΝ·Ϥ	Ϥ·ΝΑ·ΤΟΥΧΕ·ΤΗΥΤΝ		ΕϢϢ-
which-have-you(pl)-him,	he-will-save-yourselves;	>	i-
-ΠΕ	ΜΝ·ΤΗ·ΤΝ·ΠΗ	2Ν[·ΤΗΥΤ]Ν	ΠΑΕΙ ΕΤΕ
-f	not-have-you(pl)-that-one	in-you(pl),	the-one which
ΜΝ·ΤΗ·ΤΝ·Ϥ	2Ν·ΤΗΝΕ	Ϥ[·ΝΑ·Μ]ΟΥΤ·ˋ·ΤΗΝΕ	
not-have-you(pl)-him	in-you(pl),	he-will-kill- \ -you(pl).	

Jesus said, "That which you have will save you if you bring it forth from yourselves. That which you do not have within you [will] kill you if you do not have it within you."

INTERPRETATION:

His grace and truth are messages that must remain generic teachings and be activated when we believe them with all our hearts. Thus, His Kingdom dwells within us. Moreover, His guidance and grace for our lives flow from within us.

It is the reality of all those who are united to the Father. God within us is the very essence of our resurrection life.

Not having Christ within us and not making our hearts His Tabernacle will lead us to death, for there is no life without Christ.

71

ПЄХЄ·ΙC	ХЄ	†·ΝΑ·ϢΟΡ[ϢⲢ̄	Μ̄·ΠЄЄΙ·Η]ЄΙ
Said Jesus	this:	I-will-destroy	this-house,

ΑΥϢ	ΜⲚ̄·ΛΑΑΥ	·ΝΑϢ·ΚΟΤ·Ϥ	[ΑΝ	Ⲛ̄·ΚЄ·CΟΠ]
and	no-one	can-build-him,	not	another-time.

Jesus said, "I shall [destroy this] house, and no one will be able to build it [. . .]" again.

INTERPRETATION:

The saying is analogous to

Mark 14:58

"We heard Him say, 'I will destroy this temple made with hands, and within three days, I will build another made without hands.'"

Jesus states this about removing the Temple of the old covenant to establish the new in man's heart.

Along with this verse, Jesus calls us back to the edification of the spirit and not to anything man-made. In a spiritual sense, the past needs to be destroyed for the new and His resurrection life to dwell in us.

72

[ⲡⲉⲝⲉ·ⲟⲩ·ⲣⲱⲙⲉ ⲛⲁ·ϥ`] ⲝⲉ ·ⲝⲟ·ⲟⲥ ⲛ̄·ⲛⲁ·ⲥⲛⲏⲩ
Said-a-man   to-him   this: "Speak   to-my-brothers

ϣⲓⲛⲁ ⲉⲩ·ⲛ[ⲁ·ⲡ]ⲱϣⲉ ⲛ̄·ⲛ̄·ϩⲛⲁⲁⲩ ⲙ̄·ⲡⲁ·ⲉⲓⲱⲧ`
so   they-may-divide   the-belongings   of-my-father

ⲛⲙ̄ⲙⲁ·ⲉⲓ ⲡⲉⲝⲁ·ϥ ⲛⲁ·ϥ` ⲝⲉ ⲱ ⲡ·ⲣⲱⲙⲉ ⲛⲓⲙ
with-me." > Said-he   to-him   this: "O   man,   who

ⲡⲉ ⲛ̄ⲧⲁϩ·ⲁ·ⲁⲧ` ⲛ̄·ⲣⲉϥ·ⲡⲱϣⲉ ⲁϥ·ⲕⲟⲧ·ϥ̄ ⲁ·`
is-he has-made-me   a-divider?"   > He-turned() to-

·ⲛⲉϥ·ⲙⲁⲑⲏⲧⲏⲥ ⲡⲉⲝⲁ·ϥ ⲛⲁ·ⲩ ⲝⲉ ⲙⲏ ⲉ·ⲉⲓ·
-his-disciples.   Said-he   to-them this: "Truly, do-I-

·ϣⲟⲟⲡ` ⲛ̄·ⲣⲉϥ·`·ⲡⲱϣⲉ
-exist   as-a- \-divider?"

[A man said] to him, "Tell my brothers to divide my father's possessions with me." He said to him, "O man, who has made me a divider?" He turned to his disciples and said to them, "I am not a divider, am I?"

INTERPRETATION:

It is analogous to

Luke 12:13-21

"Then one from the crowd said to Him, 'Teacher, tell my brother to divide the inheritance with me.' But He said to him, 'Man, who made Me a judge or an arbitrator over you?' And He said to them, 'Take heed and beware of covetousness, for one's life does not consist in the abundance of the things he possesses.' Then He spoke a parable to them, saying: 'The ground of a certain rich man yielded plentifully. And he thought within himself, saying, 'What shall I do, since I have no room to store my crops?' So, he said, 'I will do this: I will pull down my barns and build greater, and there I will store all my crops and my goods. And I will say to my soul, 'Soul, you have many goods laid up for many years; take your ease; eat, drink, and be merry.' But God said to him, 'Fool! This night your soul will be required of you; then whose will those things be which you have provided?' So is he who lays up treasure for himself and is not rich toward God."

Jesus highlights a Kingdom that is not of this world with limitless treasures. He came to give us the most wonderful inheritance our Father had for us from before the world ever was. However, to receive it, we need to take our eyes off the riches of this world.

73

ΠΕΧΕ·ΙC ΧΕ Π·Ω2C
Said Jesus this: the-harvest

ΜΕΝ ·ΝΑϢΩ·ϥ Ν·ΕΡΓΑΤΗC ΔΕ COBK ·CONC
indeed is-plentiful; the-laborers, hwvr, small(few); pray

ΔΕ Μ·Π·ΧΟΕΙC ϢΙΝΑ Εϥ·ΝΑ·ΝΕΧ·Ϥ·ΕΡΓΑΤΗC
hwvr, to-the-Lord so he-might-send- \ -laborers

ΕΒΟΛ Ε·Π·Ω2C
out to-the-harvest

Jesus said, "The harvest is great but the labourers are few. Beseech the lord, therefore, to send out labourers to the harvest."

INTERPRETATION:

The passage is analogous to

Matthew 9:37-38

"Then He said to His disciples, 'The harvest truly is plentiful, but the laborers are few. Therefore, pray the Lord of the harvest to send out laborers into His harvest.'"

74

ΠΕΧΑ·ϥ ΧΕ Π·ΧΟΕΙC ΟΥΝ·
Said-he this: " ()Lord, there-are-

·2Α2 Μ·Π·ΚΩΤΕ Ν·Τ·ΧΩΤΕ ΜΝ·ΛΑΑΥ ΔΕ 2Ν·
-many (around) the-fountain; no-thing, hwvr, in-

·Τ·ϢΩΝΕ
-the-(cistern).

He said, "O lord, there are many around the drinking trough, but there is nothing in the cistern."

Many thirsts for God but search in fountains of religious forms without water.

The Samaritan woman in John 4 was thirsty but sought water in a well that could not satisfy her. Jesus alone has living waters, of which those who drink will never thirst again.

John 4:13-15

"Jesus answered and said to her, 'Whoever drinks of this water will thirst again, but whoever drinks of the water that I shall give him will never thirst. But the water that I shall give him will become in him a fountain of water springing up into everlasting life.' The woman said to Him, 'Sir, give me this water, that I may not thirst, nor come here to draw.'"

75

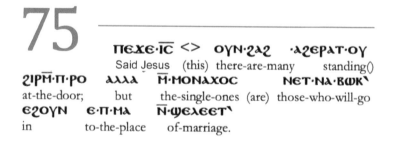

ΠⲈⲬⲈ·ⲒⲤ <> ⲞⲨⲚ·ⲈⲀⲈ ·ⲀⲈⲈⲢⲀⲦ·ⲞⲨ
Said Jesus (this) there-are-many standing()
ⲈⲒⲢⲘ·Π·ⲢⲞ ⲀⲖⲖⲀ Ⲙ·ⲘⲞⲚⲀⲬⲞⲤ ⲚⲈⲦ·ⲚⲀ·ⲂⲰⲔ
at-the-door; but the-single-ones (are) those-who-will-go
ⲈⲈⲞⲨⲚ Ⲉ·Π·ⲘⲀ Ⲛ·ϢⲈⲖⲈⲈⲦ
in to-the-place of-marriage.

Jesus said, "Many are standing at the door, but it is the solitary who will enter the bridal chamber."

INTERPRETATION:

The passage is comparable with

Song of Songs 6:8-9

"There are sixty queens and eighty concubines and virgins without number. My dove, my perfect one, is the only one, the only one of her mother, the favorite of the one who bore her. The daughters saw her and called her blessed. The queens and the concubines and they praised her."

The solitary refers to those set apart for the Lord, who have found their first great love in Him and not in anyone or anything else. They are the ones that He calls to his bridal chambers.

76

ⲠⲈⲬⲈ·ⲒⲤ ⲬⲈ
Said Jesus   this:

Ⲧ·ⲘⲚⲦⲈⲢⲟ	Ⲙ·Ⲡ·ⲈⲒⲰⲦˋ	ⲈⲤ·ⲦⲚⲦⲰⲚ	Ⲁ·Ⲩ·ⲢⲰⲘⲈ
the-kingdom	of-the-father,	she-compares	to-a-man
Ⲛ·ⲈϢⲰⲦˋ	ⲈⲨⲚ·ⲦⲀ·ϥˋ	Ⲙ·ⲘⲀⲨ	Ⲛ·ⲞⲨ·ⲪⲞⲢⲦⲒ-
of-trade	having-he	there	a-consign-
-ⲞⲚ	Ⲉ·Ⲁϥ·ⲌⲈ	Ⲁ·Ⲩ·ⲘⲀⲢⲄⲀⲢⲒⲦⲎⲤ	Ⲡ·ⲈϢⲰⲦˋ
-ment;	he-fell	upon-a-pearl;	> the-trader
ⲈⲦ·Ⲙ·ⲘⲀⲨ	ⲞⲨ·ⲤⲀⲂⲈ	ⲠⲈ	Ⲁϥ·Ⲧⲓ·ⲠⲈ·ⲪⲞⲢⲦⲒⲞⲚ
who-was-there,	a-wise-one	was(he);	he-gave-the-consignment
ⲈⲂⲞⲖ	Ⲁϥ·ⲦⲞⲞⲨ	ⲚⲀ·ϥˋ	Ⲙ·Ⲡⲓ·ⲘⲀⲢⲄⲀⲢⲒⲦⲎⲤ
away;	he-bought	for-him (self)	that-pearl
ⲞⲨⲰⲦˋ	Ⲛ·ⲦⲰ·ⲦⲚ	ⲌⲰⲦˋ·ⲦⲎⲨⲦⲚ	·ϢⲒⲚⲈ Ⲛ-
alone.	> You(pl),	also- \-yourselves,	seek af-
-ⲤⲀ·ⲠⲈϥ·ⲈⲌⲞ	Ⲉ·ⲘⲀϥ·ⲰⲬⲚ	Ⲉϥ·ⲘⲎⲚˋ	ⲈⲂⲞⲖ
-ter-his-treasure	that-does-not()perish,	()enduring	out;
Ⲡ·ⲘⲀ	Ⲉ·ⲘⲀ·ⲢⲈ·ⲬⲞⲞⲖⲈⲤ	·ⲦⲌⲚⲞ	ⲈⲌⲞⲨⲚˋ Ⲉ·ⲘⲀⲨ
the-place	where-no-moth	approaches	in to-there
Ⲉ·ⲞⲨⲰⲘˋ	ⲞⲨⲆⲈ	ⲘⲀ·ⲢⲈϥ·ϧⲚⲦ	·ⲦⲀⲔⲞ
to-eat,	&nor	no-worms	destroy.

Jesus said, "The kingdom of the father is like a merchant who had a consignment of merchandise and who discovered a pearl. That merchant was shrewd. He sold the merchandise and bought the pearl alone for himself. You too, seek his unfailing and enduring treasure where no moth comes near to devour and no worm destroys."

INTERPRETATION:

The passage is analogous to

Matthew 13:45–46

"Again, the kingdom of heaven is like a merchant seeking beautiful pearls, who, when he had found one pearl of great price, went and sold all that he had and bought it."

Jesus is the pearl of great price, worth selling everything to have Him.

Thomas expands the view, indicating that the eternal treasures, 'the treasures of his countenance,' have to do with knowing the face of Christ, beholding Him, going deeper into Him, and living before Him.

77

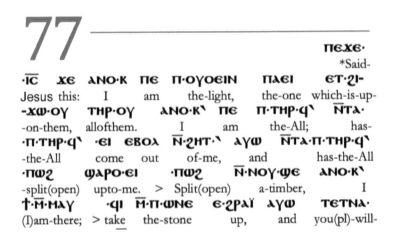

ΠΕΧΕ·
*Said-

·ⲓⲥ ⲭⲉ ⲁⲛⲟⲕ ⲡⲉ ⲡ·ⲟⲩⲟⲉⲓⲛ ⲡⲁⲉⲓ ⲉⲧ·ϩⲓ-
Jesus this: I am the-light, the-one which-is-up-

-ⲭⲱ·ⲟⲩ ⲧⲏⲣ·ⲟⲩ ⲁⲛⲟ·ⲕ ⲡⲉ ⲡ·ⲧⲏⲣ·ϥ ⲛ̅ⲧⲁ·
-on-them, allofthem. I am the-All; has-

·ⲡ·ⲧⲏⲣ·ϥ ·ⲉⲓ ⲉⲃⲟⲗ ⲛ̅·ϩⲏⲧ· ⲁⲩⲱ ⲛ̅ⲧⲁ·ⲡ·ⲧⲏⲣ·ϥ
-the-All come out of-me, and has-the-All

·ⲡⲱϩ ϣⲁⲣⲟ·ⲉⲓ ·ⲡⲱϩ ⲛ̅·ⲛⲟⲩ·ϣⲉ ⲁⲛⲟ·ⲕ
-split(open) upto-me. > Split(open) a-timber, I

ϯ·ⲙ̅·ⲙⲁⲩ ·ϥⲓ ⲙ̅·ⲡ·ⲱⲛⲉ ⲉ·ϩⲣⲁⲓ ⲁⲩⲱ ⲧⲉⲧⲛⲁ·
(I)am-there; > take the-stone up, and you(pl)-will-

Jesus said, "It is I who am the light which is above them all. It is I who am the all. From me did the all come forth, and unto me did the all extend. Split a piece of wood, and I am there. Lift up the stone, and you will find me there."

Jesus points out His presence is everywhere, as the Light shines on every man. He was removing the Tabernacle from the outside, establishing it inside each of us, and making us see that all things came from Him and will return to Him. Jesus is within and around us. He is the totality, the Oneness.

Or just as the Apostle Paul states in:

Colossians 1:16-17

"For by Him all things were created that are in heaven and that are on earth, visible and invisible, whether thrones or dominions or principalities or powers. All things were created through Him and for Him. And He is before all things, and in Him all things consist."

78

ⲡⲉⲝⲉ·ⲓⲤ ⲭⲉ ⲉⲧⲃⲉ·ⲟⲩ
Said Jesus   this: Because-of-what

ⲁⲧⲉⲧⲛ̄·ⲉⲓ ⲉⲃⲟⲗ ⲉ·ⲧ·ⲥⲱϣⲉ ⲉ·ⲛⲁⲩ ⲉ·ⲩ·ⲕⲁϣ
did-you(pl)-come out to-the-field? To-look at-a-reed

ⲉϥ·ⲕⲓⲙ [ⲉⲃⲟⲗ] ϩⲓⲧⲙ̄·ⲡ·ⲧⲏⲩ ⲁⲩⲱ ⲉ·ⲛⲁⲩ
()moving about by-means-of-the-wind? > And to-look

ⲉ·ⲩ·ⲣ[ⲱⲙⲉ ⲉⲩ]ⲛ̄·ϣⲧⲏⲛ ⲉⲩ·ϭⲏⲛ ϩⲓⲱ·ⲱⲃ
at-a-man having-garments ()soft upon-him(?),

[ⲛ̄·ⲑⲉ ⲛ̄·ⲛⲉⲧⲛ̄·]ⲣ̄ⲣⲱⲟⲩ ⲙⲛ̄·ⲛⲉⲧⲙ̄·ⲙⲉⲅⲓ-
like your(pl)-kings and-your(pl)-power-

-ⲥⲧⲁⲛⲟⲥ ⲛⲁⲉⲓ ⲉ·ⲛ[ⲉ·ϣⲧⲏ]ⲛ ⲉ[ⲧ·]
-ful-ones? > These (are?) in-garments which-are-

·ϭⲏⲛ ϩⲓⲱ·ⲟⲩ ⲁⲩⲱ ⲥⲉ·[ⲛⲁ]ϣ·ⲥ̄ⲥⲟⲟⲩⲛ·
-soft upon-them, and they-can-know-

·ⲧ·ⲙⲉ ⲁⲛ
-the-truth not.

Jesus said, "Why have you come out into the desert? To see a reed shaken by the wind? And to see a man clothed in fine garments [like your] kings and your great men? Upon them are the fine garments, and they are unable to discern the truth."

INTERPRETATION:

The passage is analogous in many ways to

 Matthew 11:7-9

"As they departed, Jesus began to say to the multitudes concerning John: 'What did you go out into the wilderness to see? A reed shaken by the wind? But what did you go out to see? A man clothed in soft garments? Indeed, those who wear soft clothing are in kings'

houses. But what did you go out to see? A prophet? Yes, I say to you, and more than a prophet."

79

ΠΕΧΕ·ΟΥ·ϹϩΙΜ[Ε] ΝΑ·Ϥ ϩΜ·
Said-a-woman   to-him   in-

·Π·ΜΗϢΕ ΧΕ ΝΕΕΙΑΤ[·Ϲ Ν·]ΘϩΗ Ν·
-the-crowd   this: "Blessed(is)she,   the-belly   wh-

·ΤΑϩ·ϤΙ ϩΑΡΟ·Κ ΑΥϢ Ν·ΚΙΒΕ ΕΝΤΑϩ·
-ich-bore   under-you(sg),   and   the-breasts   which-

·ϹΑΝΟΥϢ·Κ ΠΕΧΑ·Ϥ ΝΑ[·Ϲ] ΧΕ ΝΕ·
-nourished-you(sg)."   > Said-he   to-her   this: Bles-

·ΕΙΑΤ·ΟΥ Ν·ΝΕΝΤΑϩ·ϹϢΤΜ Α·ʼ
-sed(are)they,   ()-who-have-listened   to-

·Π·ΛΟΓΟϹ Μ·Π·ΕΙϢΤ ΑΥ·ΑΡΕϩ ΕΡΟ·Ϥ
-the-word   of-the-father;   they-have-watched   over-him

ϩΝ·ΟΥ·ΜΕ ΟΥΝ·ϩΝ·ϩΟΟΥ ΓΑΡ ·ΝΑ·ϢϢΠΕ
(truly),   > (for) (there-are)some-days,   (---),   will-come-to-be

ΝΤΕΤΝ·ΧΟ·ΟϹ ΧΕ ΝΕΕΙΑΤ·Ϲ Ν·ΘΗ ΤΑ·
&-you(pl)(will)speak   this-   "Blessed-is-she,   the-belly   the-

·ΕΙ ΕΤΕ ΜΠϹ·Ϣ ΑΥϢ Ν·ΚΙΒΕ ΝΑΕΙ Ε·ΜΠΟΥ·
-one which did-not-conceive, and the-breasts, these which-did-not-

·Ϯ·ΕΡϢΤΕ
-give-milk."

A woman from the crowd said to him, "Blessed are the womb which bore you and the breasts which nourished you." He said to [her], "Blessed are those who have heard the word of the father and have truly kept it. For there will be days when you (pl.) will say, 'Blessed are the womb which has not conceived and the breasts which have not given milk.' "

INTERPRETATION:

The first part of this passage is analogous to

 Luke 11:27-28
"And it happened, as He spoke these things, that a certain woman from the crowd raised her voice and said to Him, 'Blessed is the womb that bore You, and the breasts which nursed You!' But He said, 'More than that, blessed are those who hear the word of God and keep it!'"

The second part refers to the great judgment that would come during the wars of the Jews between the years 66 and 70 AD, and which Jesus prophesied in Matthew 24:19-21.

"But woe to those who are pregnant and to those who are nursing babies in those days! And pray that your flight may not be in winter or on the Sabbath. For then there will be great tribulation, such as has not been since the beginning of the world until this time, no, nor ever shall be."

Concerning this unparalleled tribulation, Flavius Josephus wrote, giving testimony of how mothers went so far as to eat their babies because of the terrible famine during the siege of Jerusalem.

80

ⲡⲉⲝⲉ·ⲓ̄ⲥ̄   ⲝⲉ   ⲡⲉⲛⲧⲁⲅ·ⲥⲟⲩⲱⲛ·
Said Jesus   this: Whoever-has-known-

·ⲡ·ⲕⲟⲥⲙⲟⲥ   ⲁⲅ·ⲅⲉ   ⲉ·ⲡ·ⲥⲱⲙⲁ   ⲡⲉⲛⲧⲁⲅ·ⲅⲉ
-the-world,   he-has-fallen upon-the-body;   > whoever-has-fallen,

ⲁⲉ   ⲉ·ⲡ·ⲥⲱⲙⲁ   ⲡ·ⲕⲟⲥⲙⲟⲥ   ·ⲙ̄ⲡϣⲁ   ⲙ̄·ⲙⲟ·ϥ`
hwvr,   upon-the-body,   the-world   be-worthy   of-him

ⲁⲛ`
not.

Jesus said, "He who has recognized the world has found the body, but he who has found the body is superior to the world."

INTERPRETATION:

Similar to verse 56.

81

ⲡⲉⲝⲉ·ⲓ̄ⲥ̄   ⲝⲉ   ⲡⲉⲛⲧⲁⲅ·ⲣ̄·ⲣⲙ̄·ⲙⲁⲟ   ⲙⲁ-
Said Jesus   this: whoever-has-become-rich,   let-

-ⲣⲉϥ·ⲣ̄·ⲣⲡⲟ   ⲁⲩⲱ   ⲡⲉⲧ·ⲉⲩⲛ̄·ⲧⲁ·ϥ`   ⲛ̄·ⲟⲩ·ⲁⲩⲛⲁ-
-him-become-king,   > and   he-who-has-he   (a)pow-

-ⲙⲓⲥ   ⲙⲁⲣⲉϥ·ⲁⲣⲛⲁ
-er,   let-him-abdicate.

Jesus said, "Let him who has grown rich be king, and let him who possesses power renounce it."

INTERPRETATION:

In a natural sense, wealth carries with it a responsibility in the eyes of God. To reign implies mercy, helping others in their needs, and being a just steward of the possessions God bestows on us. In the Gospel of Luke, we see how God rewards the one who is just with unjust riches and can receive the true wealth and what belongs to him. However, the unjust one cannot receive these things.

Luke 16:10-12

"He who is faithful in what is least is faithful also in much, and he who is unjust in what is least is unjust also in much. Therefore if you have not been faithful in the unrighteous mammon, who will commit to your trust the true riches? And if you have not been faithful in what is another man's, who will give you what is your own?"

In a spiritual sense, fully attaining the riches of understanding hidden in Christ leads us to reign with Him.

The second part of the verse alludes to the power the world or human strength has to offer, which only leads to destruction.

The power that comes from God is given to us by grace, not by our strength, and is only for His glory. Moreover, it makes us walk in humbleness, knowing that it is in our weakness that He is made perfect and wherein He manifests Himself.

2 Corinthians 12:9

"And He said to me, "My grace is sufficient for you, for My strength is made perfect in weakness." Therefore, most gladly, I will rather boast in my infirmities that the power of Christ may rest upon me."

| ΠΕΧΕ·ΙC | ΧΕ | ΠΕΤ·2ΗΝ |
| Said Jesus | this: | He-who-is-close |

ΕΡΟ·ΕΙ	ΕϤ·2ΗΝ	Ε·Τ·ϹΑΤΕ	ΑΥШ	ΠΕΤ·ΟΥΗΥ'
to-me,	he-is-close	to-the-fire,	> and	he-who-is-far
Μ·ΜΟ·ΕΙ	Ϥ·ΟΥΗΥ	Ν·Τ·ΜΝΤΕΡΟ		
from-me,	he-is-far	from-the-kingdom.		

Jesus said, "He who is near me is near the fire, and he who is far from me is far from the kingdom."

INTERPRETATION:

Jesus is the unaltered nature of the Father, made into flesh. His nature is Light, the Light that radiates, exposes, and gives us life. He is a 'consuming fire.' To come to Him is to be exposed to that Light and be willing to be purified by that fire. There is no room for anything defiled in God's Kingdom, which is Jesus Christ.

83

ΧΕ	Ν·2ΙΚωΝ	CE·ΟΥΟΝ2	ΕΒΟλ	Μ·Π·Ρω-
this:	the-images,	they-are-revealed	forth	to-the-ma-
-ΜΕ	λΥω	Π·ΟΥΟΕΙΝ	ΕΤ·Ν·2ΗΤ·ΟΥ	Ч·2ΗΠ`
-n,	and	the-light	which-is-in-them,	he-is-hidden
2Ν·ΘΙΚωΝ	Μ·Π·ΟΥΟΕΙΝ	Μ·Π·ΕΙωΤ`	Ч·Νλ·	
in-the-image	of-the-light	of-the-father;	> he-will-	
·ϬωλΠ`	ΕΒΟλ	λΥω	ΤΕЧ·2ΙΚωΝ	·2ΗΠ`
-be-revealed	forth,	and	his-image	hidden
ΕΒΟλ	2ΙΤΝ·ΠΕЧ·`·ΟΥΟΕΙΝ			
away	by-his- \ -light.			

Jesus said, "The images are manifest to man, but the light in them remains concealed in the image of the light of the father. He will become manifest, but his image will remain concealed by his light."

INTERPRETATION:

Images represent the form of our human nature. When Adam and his wife fell into sin, they lost the image of God, and their eyes were opened to see the bare natural world. They realized they were naked as they looked at their image, which had become just a mere outward form of their being.

The light of life was left concealed behind the veil of the flesh.

When the true light is revealed, and the veil of a person's inner temple is torn away, the Light of Christ wraps their fallen nature so that the Father only sees Him.

84

ⲡⲉϫⲉ·ⲓ̅ⲥ̅ <> ⲛ̅·ⲍⲟ-
Said Jesus (this) the-da-

-ⲟⲩ ⲉⲧⲉⲧⲛ̅·ⲛⲁⲩ ⲉ·ⲡⲉⲧⲛ̅·ⲉⲓⲛⲉ ⲱⲁⲣⲉⲧⲛ̅·
-ys you(pl)-look at-your(pl)-resemblance, do-you(pl)-

·ⲣⲁϣⲉ ⲍⲟⲧⲁⲛ ⲇⲉ ⲉⲧⲉⲧⲛ̅·ⲱⲁⲛ·ⲛⲁⲩ
-rejoice; > when, hwvr, you(pl)-should-look

ⲁ·ⲛⲉⲧⲛ̅·ⲍⲓⲕⲱⲛ ⲛ̅ⲧⲁⲍ·ϣⲱⲡⲉ ⲍⲓ·ⲧⲉⲧⲛ̅·ⲉ-
upon-your(pl)-images, which-come-into-being upon-your-begin-

-ⲍⲏ ⲟⲩⲧⲉ ⲙⲁⲩ·ⲙⲟⲩ ⲟⲩⲧⲉ ⲙⲁⲩ·ⲟⲩⲱⲛⲍ
-ning, n/nor do-not-they-die, n/nor do-not-they-appear

ⲉⲃⲟⲗ ⲧⲉⲧⲛⲁ·ϭⲓ ⲍⲁ·ⲟⲩⲏⲣ
forth, you(pl)-will-bear under-how-much?

Jesus said, "When you see your likeness, you rejoice. But when you see your images which came into being before you, and which neither die nor become manifest, how much you will have to bear!"

INTERPRETATION:

Man rejoices to see his appearance in this world. Our carnal nature likes to look good. Yet, here Jesus introduces our divine nature, our true image before God seated with Christ in heavenly places.

When we truly realize who we are and the glory bestowed upon us before the foundation of the world, our natural mind cannot conceive or process it, for it is vastly excellent.

Ephesians 2:4-7

"But God, who is rich in mercy, because of His great love with which He loved us, even when we were dead in trespasses, made us alive together with Christ (by grace you have been saved), and raised us together, and made us sit together in the heavenly places in Christ Jesus, that in the ages to come He might show the exceeding riches of His grace in His kindness toward us in Christ Jesus."

85

ⲡⲉⲭⲉ·ⲓ̅ⲥ̅ ⲭⲉ
Said Jesus this:

ⲛ̅ⲧⲁ·ⲁⲇⲁⲙ	·ϣⲱⲡⲉ	ⲉⲃⲟⲗ	ⲉ̅ⲛ·ⲛⲟⲩ·ⲛⲟ̅ϭ
Has-Adam	come-into-being	out	of-a-great
ⲛ̅·ⲇⲩⲛⲁⲙⲓⲥ	ⲙ̅ⲛ·ⲟⲩ·ⲛⲟ̅ϭ		ⲙ̅·ⲙ̅ⲛ̅ⲧ·ⲣ̅ⲙ̅·ⲙⲁ-
power	and-a-great		rich-
-ⲟ	ⲁⲩⲱ	ⲙ̅ⲡⲉϥ·ϣⲱⲡⲉ	ⲉ[ϥ·ⲙ̅ⲡ]ϣⲁ	ⲙ̅·ⲙⲱ·
-ness,	and	did-not-he-come-to-be	()worthy	of-you-
·ⲧⲛ̅	ⲛⲉ·ⲩ·ⲁⲝⲓⲟⲥ	ⲅⲁⲣ	ⲡⲉ	[ⲛⲉϥ·ⲛⲁ·ⲭⲓ·ⲧⲡⲉ]
-(pl),	>(for) had-they!deserving	(---)	(been),	he-would-have-tasted
ⲁⲛ	ⲙ̅·ⲡ·ⲙⲟⲩ			
not	(the)Death.			

Jesus said, "Adam came into being from a great power and a great wealth, but he did not become worthy of you. For had he been worthy, [he would] not [have experienced] death."

INTERPRETATION:

Out of all the gospels, this is the only saying where we see Jesus naming Adam. Later Paul would go on to explain the work of Christ as the last Adam in detail, or in other words, as the ultimate human (1 Corinthians 15:22-45).

Following the line of the sayings of Jesus compiled by Thomas, we must interpret this mention of Adam as 'humanity' and not only as a male.

So this Adam (male and female) came from the abundant wealth and power of his eternal origin in God. But humankind did not show its dignity by abstaining from eating from the tree of the knowledge of good and evil but tasted it, thereby becoming dead to the wealth and power from which they proceeded. (Genesis 2:7)

86

ΠΕΧΕ·ΙC   Χ|Є   Ν·ΒΑϢΟΡ   ΟΥ]-
Said Jesus___   this: the-foxes   hav-
-[Ν·ΤΑ·]Υ·Ν[ΟΥ·ΒΗΒ]   ΑΥϢ   Ν·ϩΑλλΑΤЄ   ΟΥΝ·ΤΑ·Υ
-e-they-their-dens,   and   the-birds   have-they
Μ·ΜΑΥ   Μ·[ΠΟ]Υ·ΜΑϩ   Π·ϢΗΡЄ   ΔЄ   Μ·Π·ΡϢΜЄ
there   their-nest;   >   the-son,   hwvr,   of-the-man,
ΜΝ·ΤΑ·ϥ`   Ν·[ΝΟΥ]ΜΑ   Є·ΡΙΚЄ   Ν·ΤЄϥ·`·ΑΠЄ   Νϥ·`
has-not-he   a-place   to-lay   his- \ -head   &()-
·ΜΤΟΝ`   Μ[ΜΟ]·ϥ`
-rest   him(self).

Jesus said, "[The foxes have their holes] and the birds have their nests, but the son of man has no place to lay his head and rest."

INTERPRETATION:

The saying is analogous to Matthew 8:20 and Luke 9:58.

Matthew 8:20

"And Jesus said to him, "Foxes have holes and birds of the air have nests, but the Son of Man has nowhere to lay His head."

In this case, Jesus' words are linked to saying #87 of this gospel. Until then, the "head" of the church and the place of His rest had not been established among men. God's house at that time, the Temple, had ceased to be where God rested and became a corrupt, worldly, religious system. It was to this fallen Judaism whom Jesus referred to as foxes.

Luke 13:31-32 and 34-35

"That same day, some of the proud religious law-keepers came to Jesus. They said, 'Go away from here! Herod wants to kill You.' Jesus said to them, 'Go and tell that fox, See. I put out demons and heal the sick. I will do these things today and tomorrow. And on the third day, My work will be finished. Jerusalem, Jerusalem, you kill the early preachers and throw stones at those sent to you. How many times I wanted to gather your children around me, as a bird gathers her young under her wings, but you would not let Me. See! Your house is empty. And I tell you, you will not see Me again until the time comes when you will say: Great and honored is the One Who comes in the name of the Lord.'"

That is why it says, "that foxes have their holes."

Once the church was established, Christ had a place to lie down and settle. He is the husband and the head of that living body (Ephesians 4:15 and 5:23 - Colossians 1:18).

At the same time, the church would be God's new dwelling place on earth, and illegitimate Herod's temple (the hole of the foxes) in the year 70 AD.

87

ⲡⲉⲝⲁ·ϥ   ⲛ̄ϭⲓ·ⲓ̄ⲥ̄   ⲝⲉ   ⲟⲩ·ⲧⲁⲗⲁⲓ-
Said-he,   viz-Jesus   this: a-wretch-
-ⲡⲱⲣⲟⲛ`   ⲡ[ⲉ]   ⲡ·ⲥⲱⲙⲁ   ⲉⲧ·ⲁϣⲉ   ⲛ̄·ⲟⲩ·ⲥⲱⲙⲁ`
-ed-one   is-he,   the-body   which-depends   on-a-body,
ⲁⲩⲱ   ⲟⲩ·ⲧ[ⲁ]ⲗⲁⲓⲡⲱⲣⲟⲥ   ⲧⲉ   ⲧ·`ⲯⲩⲭⲏ   ⲉⲧ·ⲁϣⲉ
and   a-wretched-one   is-she,   the-\ -soul   which-depends
ⲛ̄·ⲛⲁⲉⲓ   ⲙ̄·ⲡ·ⲥⲛⲁⲩ
on-these,   the-two.

Jesus said, "Wretched is the body that is dependent upon a body, and wretched is the soul that is dependent on these two."

INTERPRETATION:

By understanding saying #86, it becomes more apparent. Jesus pronounces a judgment on those who prefer to depend on the system or 'another body.'

An apparent reference to the words of Jeremiah when the prophet spoke of Judah's sin upon their decision to trust in an ungodly system.

> **Jeremiah 17:4-5**
> "And you, even yourself, shall let go of your heritage which I gave you; and I will cause you to serve your enemies in the land which you do not know, for you have kindled a fire in My anger which shall burn forever. Thus says the Lord, 'Cursed is the man who trusts in man and makes flesh his strength, whose heart departs from the Lord.'"

88

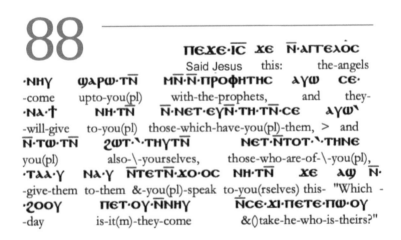

| ΠΕΧΕ·ΙC | ΧΕ | Ν·ΑΓΓΕΛΟC |
| Said Jesus | this: | the-angels |

| ·ΝΗΥ | ϢΑΡΩ·ΤΝ | ΜΝ·Ν·ΠΡΟΦΗΤΗC | ΑΥΩ | CΕ· |
| -come | upto-you(pl) | with-the-prophets, | and | they- |

| ·ΝΑ·† | ΝΗ·ΤΝ | Ν·ΝΕΤ·ΕΥΝ·ΤΗ·ΤΝ·CΕ | ΑΥΩ |
| -will-give | to-you(pl) | those-which-have-you(pl)-them, > | and |

| Ν·ΤΩ·ΤΝ | ΖΩΤ·\·ΘΗΥΤΝ | ΝΕΤ·ΝΤΟΤ·\·ΘΗΝΕ |
| you(pl) | also-\-yourselves, | those-who-are-of-\-you(pl), |

| ·ΤΑΑ·Υ | ΝΑ·Υ | ΝΤΕΤΝ·ΧΟ·ΟC | ΝΗ·ΤΝ | ΧΕ | ΑϢ | Ν· |
| -give-them | to-them | &-you(pl)-speak | to-you(rselves) | this: | "Which | - |

| ·ΖΟΟΥ | ΠΕΤ·ΟΥ·ΝΝΗΥ | ΝCΕ·ΧΙ·ΠΕΤΕ·ΠΩ·ΟΥ |
| -day | is-it(m)-they-come | &()take-he-who-is-theirs?" |

Jesus said, "The angels and the prophets will come to you and give to you those things you (already) have. And you too, give them those things which you have, and say to yourselves, 'When will they come and take what is theirs?' "

INTERPRETATION:

This is a promise together with a question mark since God had sent angels and anointed ones (prophets and wise kings) to serve Israel and announce, from time to time, the coming of the Messiah (Proverbs 16:10).

"To give to men that which was given to them." When the promised Messiah appeared, the times were fulfilled in Him, and a new era ushered in, which included a different way in which angels and the anointed ones were to operate.

It is why Jesus asks, "On what day will they come to receive their own?" referring to the day of righteousness and retribution (Luke 21:22 and 2 Thessalonians 1:6-12) when the ungodly system was destroyed in 70 AD.

In this new era of Christ, the angels could see Christ redeeming the universe and had the privilege of worshiping Him. It is a foundation of the gospel **(1 Timothy 3:16).**

 "And without controversy great is the mystery of godliness: God was manifested in the flesh, justified in the Spirit, seen by angels, preached among the Gentiles, believed on in the world, received up in glory."

It was at this time that the angels received letters for the churches, as well as incense, trumpets, cups, etc. (Rev. 2:1, Rev. 8:2-3 and Rev. 15:7). But they also received wisdom from the gospel they had not known (1 Peter 3:22) and the company of the saints made perfect (Hebrews 12:22). That day was fulfilled. Both God's anointed ones and the angels continue to receive new things.

89

ПЄХЄ·ІC	ХЄ	ЄТВЄ·ОУ	ТЄТÑ·ЄІШЄ	Ñ·П·СА·N·
Said Jesus	this:	Because-of-what	do-you(pl)-wash	the-side-
·ВОΛ`	Ñ·П·ПОТНРІОN	ТЄТÑ·Р·NОЄІ	АN	ХЄ
-outer	of-the-cup?	> Do-you(pl)-understand	not	that
ПЄNТА2·ТАМІО	Ñ·П·СА·N·2ОУN	Ñ·ТО·q	ON	
whoever-created	the-side-inner,	he	also	
ПЄNТАq·ТАМІО	Ñ·П·СА·N·ВОΛ`			
(is)he-who()created	the-side-outer?			

Jesus said, "Why do you wash the outside of the cup? Do you not realise that he who made the inside is the same one who made the outside?"

INTERPRETATION:

The passage is analogous to the rebuke given to the Pharisees in **Matthew 23:25-26**

    "Woe to you, scribes and Pharisees, hypocrites! For you cleanse the outside of the cup and dish, but inside, they are full of extortion and self-indulgence. Blind Pharisee, first cleanse the inside of the cup and dish, that the outside of them may be clean also."

90

ΠΕΧΕ·ΙC
Said Jesus

ХЄ	·АМНЄІΤΝ̄	ШАРО·ЄІ`	ХЄ	ОΥ·ΧΡΗCΤΟC
this:	Come-you(pl)	upto-me,	for	a-just-one
ΠЄ	ΠΑ·ΝΑ2Β`	ΑΥШ	ΤΑ·МΝ̄Τ·ΧΟЄΙC	ОΥ·ΡΜ̄·
is(m)	my-yoke,	and	my-Lordship	a-man-
·ΡΑШ	ΤЄ	ΑΥШ	ΤЄΤΝΑ·2Є	Α·Υ·ΑΝΑΥΠΑCΙC ΝΗ·
-gentle	is-she, >	and	you(pl)-will-fall	into-a-repose to-
·ΤΝ̄				
-you(pl).				

Jesus said, "Come unto me, for my yoke is easy and my lordship is mild, and you will find repose for yourselves."

INTERPRETATION:

The passage is analogous to

Matthew 11:29-30
"Take My yoke upon you and learn from Me, for I am gentle and lowly in heart, and you will find rest for your souls. For My yoke is easy and My burden is light."

The emphasis on the words differs in Thomas' saying, expanding on the passage's original idea in Matthew's Gospel.

By saying, "My yoke is natural," it implies that it is easy since it doesn't require any rituals, external efforts, or possessions to attain as the law did.

We are yoked with Christ. We are his spouse as a church, but his dominion over us is meek.

91

ΠΕΧΑ·Υ	ΝΑ·q`	ΧΕ	·ΧΟ·ΟC	ΕΡΟ·Ν	ΧΕ
Said-they	to-him	this:	"Speak __	to-us	this:

Ν̄ΤΚ·ΝΙΜ`	ϢΙΝΑ	ΕΝΑ·P̄·ΠΙCΤΕΥΕ	ΕΡΟ·Κ`	ΠΕ-
you(sg)(are)who,	so	we-may-believe __	you(sg)."	> Sa-

-ΧΑ·q	ΝΑ·Υ	ΧΕ	ΤΕΤΝ̄·P̄·ΠΙΡΑΖΕ	Μ̄·Π·ϨΟ	Ν̄·Τ·ΠΕ
-id-he	to-them	this:	" you(pl)-read	the-face	of-the-sky

Μ̄Ν·Π·ΚΑϨ	ΑΥШ	ΠΕΤ·Ν̄·ΠΕΤΝ̄·Μ̄ΤΟ	ΕΒΟΛ`
and-the-earth,	and	he-who-was-of-your(pl)-presence	( ),

Μ̄ΠΕΤΝ̄·COΥШΝ·q`	ΑΥШ	ΠΕΕΙ·ΚΑΙΡΟC	ΤΕ-
you(pl)-did-not-know-him, __	and	this-moment,	you-

-ΤΝ̄·ΚΟΟΥΝ	ΑΝ	Ν̄·P̄·ΠΙΡΑΖΕ	Μ̄·ΜΟ·q`
-(pl)-know	not (how)	to-read	him."

They said to him, "Tell us who you are so that we may believe in you." He said to them, "You read the face of the sky and of the earth, but you have not

recognized the one who is before you, and you do not know how to read this moment."

INTERPRETATION:

The passage is analogous to **Matthew 16:3a**

" "...and in the morning, 'It will be foul weather today, for the sky is red and threatening.' Hypocrites! You know how to discern the face of the sky, but you cannot discern the signs of the times!"

But we find Thomas here, recording one more rebuke: after waiting for the Messiah for so long and despite having him in front of them, they neither recognize nor ask him the right questions.

Moreover, as we read this, our spirit should ask itself, what questions should we ask the Father and we are not?

92

ΠΕΧΕ
Said

ĪC ΧΕ ·ϢΙΝΕ ΑΥⲰ ΤΕΤΝΑ·ϬΙΝΕ ΑΛΛΑ ΝΕ-
Jesus this: Seek, and you(pl)-will-find; > but those-

-Τ·ΑΤΕΤΝ·ΧΝΟΥ·ΕΙ ΕΡΟ·ΟΥ Ν·ΝΙ·ϨΟΟΥ Ε·ΜΠΙ·
-which-you(pl)-asked-me about-() in-those-days, I-did-not-

·ΧΟ·ΟΥ ΝΗ·ΤΝ Μ·ΦΟΟΥ ΕΤ·Μ·ΜΑΥ ΤΕΝΟΥ
-tell-them to-you(pl) in-the-day which-was-there; now,

Ε·ϨΝΑ·Ï Ε·ΧΟ·ΟΥ ΑΥⲰ ΤΕΤΝ·ϢΙΝΕ ΑΝ` ΝϹⲰ·
it-pleases-me to-tell-them, and you(pl)-seek not after-

·ΟΥ
-them.

Jesus said, "Seek and you will find. Yet, what you asked me about in former times and which I did not tell you then, now I do desire to tell, but you do not inquire after it."

It starts with a phrase that's analogous to Matthew 7:7 and Luke 11:9

 Matthew 7:7
"Ask, and it will be given to you; seek, and you will find; knock, and it will be opened to you."

Following the emphasis of the previous sayings, Jesus tells them that He can now respond to the questions that Israel has been asking for many years. But now that Christ wants them to know, they don't ask the right questions.

93

м̄п̄р̄·т·пет·оуаав   н̄·н·оу2оор`   хекас
Do-not-give-what-is-holy   to-the-dogs,   sothat(sp)

ноу·нох·оу   е·т·коприа   м̄п̄р̄·ноухе   н·м̄·
they-not-cast-them   onto-the-dungheap;   >   do-not-cast   the-

·маргарітн[с   н̄·]н·ешау   шіна хе   ноу·а·ач`
-pearls   to-the-swine,   so   that   they-not-make-him

[-]·л[---]

<Jesus said,> "Do not give what is holy to dogs, lest they throw them on the dung heap. Do not throw the pearls [to] swine, lest they ... it [...]."

The passage is analogous to **Matthew 7:6**

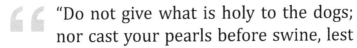 "Do not give what is holy to the dogs; nor cast your pearls before swine, lest

they trample them under their feet, and turn and tear you in pieces."

In this case, the natural and religious mind of the Pharisees cannot appreciate the truths or heavenly pearls and therefore tramples them or mixes them with their precepts and human righteousness, which in God's eyes are as filthy rags.

The word "dog" in Greek means "cynical," referring to the philosophical trends that had infested Israel, especially the one that bears this name.

94

ⲡⲉⲭⲉ·ⲓ̅ⲥ̅ <> ⲡⲉⲧ·ϣⲓⲛⲉ ϥ·ⲛⲁ·ϭⲓⲛⲉ
Said Jesus (this): He-who-seeks, he-will-find,

[ⲁⲩⲱ ⲡⲉⲧ·ⲧⲁϩⲙ· ⲉ·]ϩⲟⲩⲛ ⲥⲉ·ⲛⲁ·ⲟⲩⲱⲛ ⲛⲁ·ϥ·
and he-who-is-called in, they-will-open to-him.

Jesus [said], "He who seeks will find, and [he who knocks] will be let in."

INTERPRETATION:

The passage is analogous to Matthew 7:7 and Luke 11:9

Matthew 7:7
"Ask, and it will be given to you; seek, and you will find; knock, and it will be opened to you."

In light of the above, Jesus invites them to long to find the pearls and open the doors that had been closed up to that moment.

95

[ΠΕΧΕ·ΙC ΧΕ] ΕϢⲰΠΕ ΟΥⲚ·ΤΗ·ΤⲚ·ϨΟⲘΤ`
Said Jesus this: If have-you(pl)-money,
ⲘΠⲢ·† Ε·Τ·ⲘΗⲤⲈ ⲀⲖⲖⲀ † [ⲘⲘⲞϤ Ⲙ·]ΠⲈ[ΤⲈ]-
do-not-give (at-interest). >Rather, give it/him to-he-who-you-
-ΤⲚⲀ·ΧΙΤ·ΟΥ ⲀⲚ Ⲛ·ΤΟΟΤ·Ϥ`
-(pl)-will-take() not from-his-hand.

[Jesus said], "If you have money do not lend it at interest, but give [it] to one from whom you will not get it back."

INTERPRETATION:

The passage is similar to Jesus's words during the meal at the Pharisee ruler's house.

Luke 14:12-14
"Then He also said to him who invited Him, "When you give a dinner or a supper, do not ask your friends, your brothers, your relatives, nor rich neighbors, lest they also invite you back, and you be repaid. But when you give a feast, invite the poor, the maimed, the lame, the blind. And you will be blessed because they cannot repay you; for you shall be repaid at the resurrection of the just."

Here, Jesus again introduces the idea that His Kingdom is generous and should be lived out of generosity.

96

ΠΕΧΕ·ΙC ΧΕ Τ·ΜΝ-
Said Jesus this: the-king-

-ΤΕΡΟ Μ·Π·ΕΙϢΤ` ΕC·ΤΝΤϢ[Ν Ε·Υ·]ϾϨΙΜΕ
-dom of-the-father, she-compares to-a-woman;

ΑϾ·ΧΙ Ν·ΟΥ·ΚΟΥΕΙ Ν·ϾΑΕΙΡ [ΑϾ·ϨΟ]Π·Ϥ` ϨΝ·
she-took a-little-bit of-leaven; she-hid-it/him in-

·ΟΥ·ϢϢΤΕ ΑϾ·Α·ΑϤ Ν·ϨΝ·ΝΟ[Ϭ Ν]Ν·ΟΕΙΚ`
-(a)dough; she-made-it/him (into)some-great(loaves) of-bread.

ΠΕΤ·ΕΥΜ·ΜΑΑΧΕ Μ·ΜΟ·Ϥ ΜΑ[ΡΕϤ·]ϾϢΤΜ`
He-who-has-ear of-him, let-him-listen.

Jesus said, "The kingdom of the father is like [a certain] woman. She took a little leaven, [concealed] it in some dough, and made it into large loaves. Let him who has ears hear."

INTERPRETATION:

The passage is analogous to

Matthew 13:33
"Another parable He spoke to them: "The kingdom of heaven is like leaven, which a woman took and hid in three measures of meal till it was all leavened."

A word, a pearl, or a simple answer from Heaven can expand until it fills it all.

97

ΠΕΧΕ·ΙC ΧΕ Τ·ΜΝ̄ΤΕΡΟ Μ̄·Π·Ε[ΙΩΤ' ΕC·]ΤΝ̄-
Said Jesus this: the-kingdom of-the-father, she-com-

-ΤΩΝ Α·Υ·CϨΙΜΕ ΕC·ϬΙ ϨΑ·ΟΥ·ϬΑ[ΜΕΕΙ] ΕϤ·`
-pares to-a-woman ()bearing under-a-jar, ()-

·ΜΕϨ Ν̄·ΝΟΕΙΤ' ΕC·ΜΟΟϢΕ Ϩ[Ι·ΟΥ·]ϨΙΗ`
-full of-meal; > ()-walking on-a-road

ΕC·ΟΥΗΟΥ Α·Π·ΜΑΑΧΕ Μ̄·Π·ϬΑΜ[ΕΕΙ] ·ΟΥ-
()faraway; did-the-ear of-the-jar br-

-ΩϬΠ' Α·Π·ΝΟΕΙΤ' ·ϢΟΥΟ Ν̄CΩ·[C Ϩ Ι·]ΤΕ·ϨΙ-
-eak; did-the-meal empty(out) after-her on-the-roa-

-Η ΝΕ·C·CΟΟΥΝ ΑΝ ΠΕ ΝΕ·Μ̄ΠΕC·ΕΙΜΕ
-d; > she-knew not (it) tobe; did-not-she-realize

Ε·ϨΙCΕ Ν̄ΤΑΡΕC·ΠΩϨ ΕϨΟΥΝ Ε·ΠΕC·ΗΕΙ
a-trouble(?); > when-she-opened in to-her-house,

ΑC·ΚΑ·Π·ϬΑΜΕΕΙ Α·Π·ΕCΗΤ' ΑC·ϨΕ ΕΡΟ·Ϥ ΕϤ·`
she-put-the-jar (down); she-fell on-him, he-being-

·ϢΟΥΕΙΤ'
-empty.

Jesus said, "The kingdom of the [father] is like a certain woman who was carrying a [jar] full of meal. While she was walking [on the] road, still some distance from home, the handle of the jar broke and the meal emptied out behind her [on] the road. She did not realize it; she had noticed no accident. When she reached her house, she set the jar down and found it empty."

INTERPRETATION:

Jesus is showing the generosity of the Kingdom, which implies that the inner (the grain in the jar) is to be emptied outwardly; that a hidden pearl or treasure is to be revealed (Matthew 13:46);

that virtue is imparted to others, even if this is by accident or beyond the control of the one who possesses that grain, pearl, or treasure (2 Corinthians 4:7).

Jesus himself experienced this with the woman with the issue of blood, who, through faith, drew virtue from Christ for her healing (Mark 5:25-34).

Another possible interpretation may refer to being aware of the blessings we have received from God. Don't allow them to be accidentally lost or stolen from us, but as good stewards, we are to reach the end of our lives full of the fruit He has granted us.

98

ΠⲈⲬⲈ·ⲓⲤ	<>	Ⲧ·ⲘⲚ̅ⲦⲈⲢⲞ	Ⲙ̅·Π·ⲈⲒⲰⲦ`
Said Jesus		(this) the-kingdom	of-the-father,

ⲈⲤ·ⲦⲚ̅ⲦⲰⲚ	Ⲉ·Ⲩ·ⲢⲰⲘⲈ	ⲈϤ·ⲞⲨⲰϢ	Ⲉ·ⲘⲞⲨⲦ
she-compares	to-a-man	()wanting	to-kill-

·ⲞⲨ·ⲢⲰⲘⲈ	Ⲙ̅·ⲘⲈⲄⲒⲤⲦⲀⲚⲞⲤ	ⲀϤ·ϢⲰⲀⲘ`	Ⲛ̅·
-a-man	powerful. >	He-drew	-

·Ⲧ·ⲤⲎϤⲈ	Ϩ̅Ⲙ·ΠⲈϤ·ϨⲈⲒ	ⲀϤ·ⲬⲞⲦ·Ⲥ̅	Ⲛ̅·Ⲧ·ⲬⲞ	ⲬⲈ-
-the-sword	in-his-house;	he-stuck-her	into-the-wall,	so-

-ⲔⲀⲀⲤ	ⲈϤ·ⲚⲀ·ⲈⲒⲘⲈ	ⲬⲈ	ⲦⲈϤ·ϬⲒⳜ`	·ⲚⲀ·ⲦⲰⲔ`
-that	he-might-realize	that	his-hand	(would)-be-strong

ⲈϨⲞⲨⲚ	ⲦⲞⲦⲈ	ⲀϤ·Ϩ̅ⲰⲦⲂ̅	Ⲙ̅·Π·ⲘⲈⲄⲒⲤⲦⲀⲚⲞⲤ
inwardly(?), >	then	he-slew	the-powerful-one.

Jesus said, "The kingdom of the father is like a certain man who wanted to kill a powerful man.

In his own house he drew his sword and stuck it into the wall in order to find out whether his hand could carry through. Then he slew the powerful man."

The passage should be understood analogously to **Matthew 10:34**

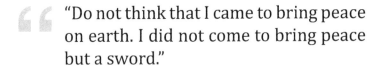 "Do not think that I came to bring peace on earth. I did not come to bring peace but a sword."

Jesus once again recalls the judgment and the sword that would come upon the system, who in this case would be the 'powerful man,' and of whom Jesus Himself prophesied in Luke 21:24 upon releasing judgment in Jerusalem.

Luke 21:24
"And they will fall by the edge of the sword and be led away captive into all nations. And Jerusalem will be trampled by Gentiles until the times of the Gentiles are fulfilled."

The Kingdom had sent its prophets as a sword in God's hand. They had declared judgment several times against the system of ungodliness maintained by the scribes, Pharisees, and Sadducees and endorsed by Herod (Edom).

(Isaiah 34:5, Jeremiah 12:12, Ezekiel 11:8-10)

The powerful man, i.e., the religious and worldly system, would be wholly overthrown by God. The ungodly house would be plundered (Matthew 12:29).

This occurred in the year 70 AD with the temple's destruction.

99 ──────────

ΠⲈⲜⲈ·Ⲙ·ⲘⲀⲐⲎⲦⲎⲤ	ⲚⲀ·ϥ	ⲜⲈ	ⲚⲈⲔ·ˋ·ⲤⲚⲎⲨ
Said-the-disciples	to-him	this:	your(sg)-\-brothers
ⲘⲚ̄·ⲦⲈⲔ·ⲘⲀⲀⲨ	ⲤⲈ·ⲀϨⲈⲢⲀⲦ·ⲞⲨ		ϨⲒ·Π·ⲤⲀ·Ⲛ·
and-your(sg)-mother,	they-are-standing()		on-the-side-
·ⲂⲞⲖ	ΠⲈⲜⲀ·ϥ	ⲚⲀ·Ⲩ	ⲜⲈ	ⲚⲈⲦ·Ⲛ̄·ⲚⲈⲈⲒ·ⲘⲀ
-outer.	> Said-he	to-them	this:	those-in-these-places
ⲈⲦⲢⲈ	Ⲙ̄·Π·ⲞⲨⲰϢ	Ⲙ̄·ΠⲀ·ⲈⲒⲰⲦˋ	ⲚⲀⲈⲒ	ⲚⲈ
who-do	the-will	of-my-father,	these	are
ⲚⲀ·ⲤⲚⲎⲨ	ⲘⲚ̄·ⲦⲀ·ⲘⲀⲀⲨ	Ⲛ̄·ⲦⲞ·ⲞⲨ	ΠⲈ	ⲈⲦ·ⲚⲀ·
my-brothers	and-my-mother; >	they	are-he	who-will
·ⲂⲰⲔˋ	ⲈϨⲞⲨⲚ	Ⲉ·Ⲧ·ⲘⲚ̄ⲦⲈⲢⲞ		Ⲙ̄·ΠⲀ·ⲈⲒⲰⲦˋ
-go	in	to-the-kingdom		of-my-father.

The disciples said to him, "Your brothers and your mother are standing outside." He said to them, "Those here who do the will of my father are my brothers and my mother. It is they who will enter the kingdom of my father."

INTERPRETATION:

The passage is analogous to

> **Matthew 12:46-50**
> "While He was still talking to the multitudes, behold, His mother and brothers stood outside, seeking to speak with Him. Then one said to Him, 'Look, Your mother and Your brothers are standing outside, seeking to speak with You.' But He answered and said to the one who told Him, 'Who is My mother, and who are My brothers?' And He stretched out His hand toward His disciples and said, 'Here are My mother and My brothers! For whoever does the will of My Father in heaven is My brother and sister and mother.'"

100 ———————————

ⲁⲩ·ⲧⲥⲉⲃⲉ·ⲓ̅ⲥ̅	ⲁ·ⲩ·ⲛⲟⲩⲃ	ⲁⲩⲱ	ⲡⲉⲝⲁ·ⲩ	ⲛⲁ·ϥ`
They-showed Jesus	a-coin,	and	said-they	to-him

ⲝⲉ	ⲛⲉⲧ·ⲏⲡ`	ⲁ·ⲕⲁⲓⲥⲁⲡ`	ⲥⲉ·ϣⲓⲧⲉ	ⲙ̅·ⲙⲟ·ⲛ	ⲛ̅·
this: "Those-who-belong	to-Caesar,	they-demand	of-us	-

·ⲛ̅·ϣⲱⲙ`	ⲡⲉⲝⲁ·ϥ	ⲛⲁ·ⲩ	ⲝⲉ	·ⲧ·ⲛⲁ·ⲕⲁⲓⲥⲁⲡ`
-the-taxes." > Said-he	to-them	this: "Give-that-of-Caesar

ⲛ̅·ⲕⲁⲓⲥⲁⲡ	·ⲧ·ⲛⲁ·ⲡ·ⲛⲟⲩⲧⲉ	ⲙ̅·ⲡ·ⲛⲟⲩⲧⲉ
to-Caesar, > give-that-of-(the)God	to-(the)God,

ⲁⲩⲱ	ⲡⲉⲧⲉ·ⲡⲱ·ⲉⲓ	ⲡⲉ	ⲙⲁ·ⲧⲛ̅ⲛⲁ·ⲉⲓ·ϥ
and	he-who-mine	is,	give-to-me(him)."

They showed Jesus a gold coin and said to him, "Caesar's men demand taxes from us." He said to them, "Give Caesar what belongs to Caesar, give

God what belongs to God, and give me what is mine."

The passage is analogous to Matthew 22:19-21 and Mark 12:14-17.

Matthew 22:19-21

"'Show Me the tax money.' So, they brought Him a denarius. And He said to them, 'Whose image and inscription is this?' They said to Him, 'Caesar's.' And He said to them, 'Render therefore to Caesar the things that are Caesar's, and to God the things that are God's.'"

101

ⲡⲉⲧⲁ·ⲙⲉⲥⲧⲉ·ⲡⲉϥ·ⲉ|ⲓⲱⲧ ⲁ|ⲛ ⲙ̄ⲛ·ⲧⲉϥ·
Whoever-hates-his-father   not,   and-his-

·ⲙⲁⲁⲩ ⲛ̄·ⲧⲁ·ϩⲉ ϥ·ⲛⲁϣ·ⲣ̄·ⲙ[ⲁⲑⲏⲧⲏ]ⲥ [ⲛⲁ·]ⲉⲓ ⲁ ̄
-mother, in-my-way,   he-can-become-disciple   to-me   not;

ⲁⲩⲱ ⲡⲉⲧⲁ·ⲙ̄ⲡ̄ⲣⲉ·ⲡⲉ[ϥ·ⲉⲓⲱⲧ ⲁⲛ ⲙ̄ⲛ·ⲧ]ⲉϥ·
and   whoever-loves-his-father   not,   and-his-

·ⲙⲁⲁⲩ ⲛ̄·ⲧⲁ·ϩⲉ ϥ·ⲛⲁϣ·ⲣ̄·ⲙ[ⲁⲑⲏⲧⲏⲥ ⲛⲁ·]
-mother,   in-my-way,   he-can-become-disciple   to-

·ⲉⲓ ⲁⲛ ⲧⲁ·ⲙⲁⲁⲩ ⲅⲁⲣ ⲛ̄ⲧⲁ[ⲥ·ⲭⲡⲉ·ⲡⲁ·ⲥⲱⲙⲁ]
-me   not; > (for) my-mother, (---),   she-begot-my-body(?)

[ⲉⲃ]ⲟⲗ [ⲧⲁ·ⲙⲁⲁⲩ] ⲇⲉ ⲙ̄·ⲙⲉ ⲁⲥ·ⲧ̄ ⲛⲁ·ⲉⲓ ·ⲡ·ⲱⲛϩ
forth;   my-mother, hwvr,   true,   she-gave   to-me   The-Life.

<Jesus said,> "Whoever does not hate his [father] and his mother as I do cannot become a [disciple]

to me. And whoever does [not] love his [father and] his mother as I do cannot become a [disciple to] me. For my mother[. . .], but [my] true [mother] gave me life." belongs to Caesar, give God what belongs to God, and give me what is mine."

INTERPRETATION:

The idea that our connection to the Kingdom exceeds our family ties is an aspect described by Jesus in the synoptic gospels. Thomas includes them here in sayings 55, 99, and 101.

The passage is also analogous to

Luke 14:26
"If anyone comes to Me and does not hate his father and mother, wife and children, brothers and sisters, yes, and his own life also, he cannot be My disciple."

Notice that he includes the concept of 'mother' to clarify that Mary would not be his mother in the spirit but only in the natural realm.

Here, Jesus introduces the idea that, as free children, we have another mother, and one can understand it in conjunction with Paul's statement in **Galatians 4:26.**

"...but the Jerusalem above is free, which is the mother of us all."

102

ΠΕΧΕ·ΙC [ΧΕ   Ο]ΥΟΕΙ   ΝΑ·Υ   Μ̄·ΦΑΡΙCΑΙΟC   ΧΕ
Said Jesus   this: Woe   to-them,   the-Pharisees,   for
ΕΥ·ΕΙΝ[Ε   Ν̄·Ν]ΟΥ·ΟΥ2ΟΡ   ΕϤ·Ν̄ΚΟΤΚ`   2ΙΧΝ̄·Π·ΟΥ-
they-resemble   a-dog   ()resting   upon-the-man-
-ΟΝΕϤ`   Ν̄·[2ΕΝ]·Ε2ΟΟΥ   ΧΕ   ΟΥΤΕ   Ϥ·ΟΥѠΜ   ΑΝ
-ger   of-some-oxen,   for   n/nor   he-eats   not
ΟΥΤΕ   Ϥ·[ΚѠ   Α]Ν   Ν̄·Ν·Ε2ΟΟΥ   Ε·ΟΥѠΜ
n/nor   he-permits not   the-oxen   to-eat.

Jesus said, "Woe to the Pharisees, for they are like a dog sleeping in the manger of oxen, for neither does he eat nor does he [let] the oxen eat."

INTERPRETATION:

The image is similar to Christ's judgment in

> **Matthew 23:13**
> "But woe to you, scribes and Pharisees, hypocrites! For you shut up the kingdom of heaven against men; for you neither go in yourselves, nor do you allow those who are entering to go in."

There is condemnation for those who, having the key, or in this case, food, neither enter nor eat nor allow others to enter or eat either.

At that time, these were the scribes, Sadducees, and Pharisees –the clerics of Judaism and the religionists of all times.

(In saying 39, Jesus refers to the clergymen and theologians who, holding the keys of knowledge, do not allow anyone to enter)

103

ⲡⲉϫⲉ·ⲓ̅ⲥ̅
Said Jesus
ϫⲉ ⲟⲩ·ⲙ[ⲁⲕⲁ]ⲣⲓⲟⲥ ⲡⲉ ⲡ·ⲣⲱⲙⲉ ⲡⲁⲉⲓ ⲉⲧ·ⲥⲟⲟⲩ¯
this: a-blessed-one is(m) the-man, the-one who-knows
ϫⲉ ϩ[ⲛ̄·ⲁϣ] ⲙ̄·ⲙⲉⲣⲟⲥ ⲉ·ⲛ·ⲗⲏⲥⲧⲏⲥ ·ⲛⲏⲩ ⲉϩⲟⲩ¯
that in-which part do-the-thieves come in,
ϣⲓⲛⲁ [ⲉϥ·ⲛ]ⲁ·ⲧⲱⲟⲩⲛ` ⲛ̄ϥ·ⲥⲱⲟⲩϩ ⲛ̄·ⲧⲉϥ·`
so he-may-arise &()-gather his-
·ⲙⲛ̄ⲧ[ⲉⲣⲟ] ⲁⲩⲱ ⲛ̄ϥ·ⲙⲟⲩⲣ ⲙ̄·ⲙⲟ·ϥ` ⲉϫⲛ̄·ⲧⲉϥ·`
-kingdom, and ()()-bind him (self) upon-his-
·ϯⲡⲉ [ϩⲁ]·ⲧ·ⲉϩⲏ ⲉⲙ`ⲡⲁⲧⲟⲩ·ⲉⲓ ⲉϩⲟⲩⲛ
-loins from-the-beginning, bef\ore-they-come in.

Jesus said, "Fortunate is the man who knows where the brigands will enter, so that [he] may get up, muster his domain, and arm himself before they invade."

INTERPRETATION:

The passage is analogous to

> **Luke 12:39-41**
>
> "'But know this, that if the master of the house had known what hour the thief would come, he would have watched and not allowed his house to be broken into. Therefore, you also be ready, for the Son of Man is coming at an hour you do not expect.' Then Peter said to Him, 'Lord, do You speak this parable only to us, or to all people?'"

104

-ⲬⲀ·Ⲩ   Ⲛ[·ⲓⲋ]   ⲬЄ   ·ⲀⲘⲞⲨ   ⲚⲦⲚ·ⲰⲖⲎⲖˋ   Ⲙ·ⲡⲞⲞⲨ
-id-they   to Jesus   this: Come(sg),   (we)-pray   today,

ⲀⲨⲰ   ⲚⲦⲚ·Ⲣ·ⲚⲎⲤⲦЄⲨЄ   ⲡЄⲬЄ·ⲓⲋ   ⲬЄ   ⲞⲨ   ⲅⲀⲢ
and   (we)-fast.   Said Jesus   this: (for) What (---),

ⲡЄ   Ⲡ·ⲚⲞⲂЄ   ⲚⲦⲀЄⲓ·Ⲁ·Ⲁϥˋ   Ⲏ   ⲚⲦⲀⲨ·ⲬⲢⲞ   ЄⲢⲞ·Єⲓ
is(m)   the-sin   I-have-done(),   or   they-have-won   over-me

Ⲍⲛ·ⲞⲨ   ⲀⲖⲖⲀ   Ⲍ̇ⲞⲦⲀⲚ   ЄⲢϢⲀⲚ·Ⲡ·ⲚⲨⲘⲫⲓⲞⲤ   ·Єⲓ
in-what?   > Rather,   when   should-the-bridegroom   come

ЄⲂⲞⲖ   Ⲍ̇Ⲙ·Ⲡ·ⲚⲨⲘⲫⲰⲚ   ⲦⲞⲦЄ   ⲘⲀⲢⲞⲨ·ⲚⲎˋ
out   of-the-bridal-chamber,   then   let-them-fa\

-ⲤⲦЄⲨЄ   ⲀⲨⲰ   ⲘⲀⲢⲞⲨ·ⲰⲖⲎⲖˋ
-st,   and   let-them-pray.

They said to Jesus, "Come, let us pray today and let us fast." Jesus said, "What is the sin that I have committed, or wherein have I been defeated? But when the bridegroom leaves the bridal chamber, then let them fast and pray."

INTERPRETATION:

The passage is similar to Matthew 9:15, Mark 2:19-20, and Luke 5:34 and 35.

Matthew 9:15

"And Jesus said to them, "Can the friends of the bridegroom mourn as long as the bridegroom is with them? But the days will come when the bridegroom will be taken away from them, and then they will fast."

Thomas adds Jesus' question, which allows us to see that fasting implies an afflicted heart seeking atonement or needing victory in some area. Something that Jesus did not need, for he was already victorious in every area and without sin.

Furthermore, in saying 27, as previously explained, Jesus speaks of fasting the system. The same thing that Clement of Alexandria emphasized in his writings.

In this passage, Jesus reveals that something dramatic will happen that will require prayer and fasting when the bridegroom steps out of the bridal chamber. "But when the bridegroom comes out of the bridal chamber, then let them fast and pray!"

We see this in Revelation 19:11-16 when Christ is joined to His Bride at the marriage supper, He rides out on a white horse to judge and bring justice.

(We understand the marriage of the lamb as when Jesus joins His Church, making her His body and inhabiting her by His Spirit).

105

ΠⲈⲬⲈ·ⲒⲤ ⲬⲈ ΠⲈ-
Said Jesus this: He-

-Ⲧ·ⲚⲀ·ⲤⲞⲨⲰⲚ·Π·ⲈⲒⲰⲦˋ ⲘⲚ·Ⲧ·ⲘⲀⲀⲨ ⲤⲈ·ⲚⲀ·ⲘⲞⲨ-
-who-will-know-the-father and-the-mother, they-will-ref-

-ⲦⲈ ⲈⲢⲞ·ϥˋ ⲬⲈ Π·ϢⲎⲢⲈ Ⲙ·ΠⲞⲢⲚⲎ
-er to-him as "the-son of(the)harlot."

Jesus said, "He who knows the father and the mother will be called the son of a harlot."

INTERPRETATION:

Before God, Israel had become a harlot, which he referred to as 'Babylon the Great,' which fornicated with idols and pagan practices. The father and mother represent the traditions and commandments of men with which Israel became defiled. In this context, the word 'know' means intimate communion, referring to those who remain rooted in a religious system, whatever it may be, as children of the harlot. (Revelation 17:1-5).

106

ΠⲈⲬⲈ·ⲒⲤ ⲬⲈ
Said Jesus this:

ⲈⲞⲦⲀⲚ ⲈⲦⲈⲦⲚ·ϢⲀ·Ⲣ·Π·ⲤⲚⲀⲨ ⲞⲨⲀ ⲦⲈⲦⲚⲀ·ϢⲰ-
when you(pl)-should-make-the-two one, you(pl)-will-come-to-

-ΠⲈ Ⲛ·ϢⲎⲢⲈ Ⲙ·Π·ⲢⲰⲘⲈ ⲀⲨⲰ ⲈⲦⲈⲦⲚ·ϢⲀⲚ·
-be the-sons of-the-man, > and if-you(pl)-should-

·ⲬⲞ·ⲞⲤ ⲬⲈ Π·ⲦⲞⲞⲨ ·ΠⲰⲰⲚⲈ ⲈⲂⲞⲖˋ ϥ·ⲚⲀ·
-speak this- "Mountain, move away," he-will-

·ΠⲰⲰⲚⲈ
-move.

Jesus said, "When you make the two one, you will become the sons of man, and when you say, 'Mountain, move away,' it will move away."

INTERPRETATION:

The passage is analogous to Jesus' saying in verse 48.

This verse, in particular, emphasizes that when we enter that oneness, beginning with the Son and the Father and subsequently with our brethren, we will be the new 'Adam.'

107

ΠΕΧΕ·ΙC	ΧΕ	Τ·ΜΝΤΕΡΟ	ΕC·ΤΝΤΩ
Said Jesus	this:	the-kingdom,	she-compares

Ε·Υ·ΡΩΜΕ	Ν·ϢΩC	ΕΥΝ·ΤΑ·Ϥ	Μ·ΜΑΥ	Ν·ϢΕ	Ν·
to-a-man	sheepherding,	who-had-he	there	100	-

·ΕCΟΟΥ	Α·ΟΥΑ	Ν·2ΗΤ·ΟΥ	·CΩΡΜ	Ε·Π·ΝΟϬ	ΠΕ
-sheep.	> Did-one	of-them	stray -	the-greatest	was-he;

ΑϤ·ΚΩ	Μ·ΠCΤΕ·ϤΙΤ	ΑϤ·ϢΙΝΕ	ΝCΑ·ΠΙ·ΟΥΑ
he-left	(the)ninety-nine;	he-sought	after-that-one

ϢΑΝΤΕϤ·2Ε	ΕΡΟ·Ϥ	ΝΤΑΡΕϤ·2ΙCΕ	ΠΕΧΑ·Ϥ
until-he-fell	upon-him;	> having-been-troubled,	said-he

Μ·Π·ΕCΟΟΥ	ΧΕ	†·ΟΥΟϢ·Κ	ΠΑΡΑ·ΠCΤΕ·ϤΙΤ
to-the-sheep	this:	"I-love/want-you(sg)	more-than(the)99."

Jesus said, "The kingdom is like a shepherd who had a hundred sheep. One of them, the largest, went astray. He left the ninety-nine and looked for that one until he found it. When he had gone to such trouble, he said to the sheep, 'I care for you more than the ninety-nine.'"

The passage is analogous to

 Matthew 18:12-14
"What do you think? If a man has a hundred sheep, and one of them goes astray, does he not leave the ninety-nine and go to the mountains to seek the one that is straying? And if he should find it, assuredly, I say to you, he rejoices more over that sheep than over the ninety-nine that did not go astray. Even so it is not the will of your Father who is in heaven that one of these little ones should perish."

But when he tells number 100, "I love you more than the 99," Thomas lets us see that the number 100 is the church composed of the converted Jews and the Gentiles.

It can be compared to what was prophesied in the song of Moses.

 Deuteronomy 32:21
"They have provoked Me to jealousy by what is not God;

They have moved Me to anger by their foolish idols. But I will provoke them to jealousy by those who are not a nation;

I will move them to anger by a foolish nation."

108

ΠⲈⲬⲈ·ⲒⲤ	ⲬⲈ	ΠⲈⲦⲀ·ⲤⲰ	ⲈⲂⲞⲖ	ⲞⲚ·ⲦⲀ·ⲦⲀΠⲢⲞ
Said Jesus	this:	Whoever-drinks	out	of-my-mouth,

Ⲥ·ⲚⲀ·ⲰⲰΠⲈ	Ⲛ·ⲦⲀ·ⲞⲈ	ⲀⲚⲞ·Ⲕ	ⲞⲰ·	Ⲧ·ⲚⲀ·ⲰⲰΠⲈ
he-will-come-to-be	in-my-way;	> I	also(I),	I-will-come-to-be

Ⲉ·ⲚⲦⲞ·Ⲋ	ΠⲈ	ⲀⲨⲰ	ⲚⲈⲐⲎΠ`	·ⲚⲀ·ⲞⲨⲰⲚⲞ	ⲈⲢⲞ·Ⲋ`
as-he	is,	> and	those-hidden	will-appear	to-him.

Jesus said, "He who will drink from my mouth will become like me. I myself shall become he, and the things that are hidden will be revealed to him."

INTERPRETATION:

Jesus emphasizes that HE is the source, and whosoever drinks from his words will be transformed. It could also be a summary of the encounter with the Samaritan woman. (John 4:9-29)

 John 4:10

"Jesus answered and said to her, 'If you knew the gift of God, and who it is who says to you, 'Give Me a drink,' you would have asked Him, and He would have given you living water.'"

109

ΠΕΧΕ·ΙC ΧΕ	Τ·ΜΝ̄ΤΕΡΟ	ΕC·ΤΝ̄ΤωΝ	Ε·Υ·Ρω-
Said Jesus this:	the-kingdom,	she-compares	to-a-ma-

-ΜΕ	ΕΥΝ̄·ΤΑ·Ϥ	[Μ̄]ΜΑΥ	2Ν̄·ΤΕϤ·`·Cω ϢΕ	Ν̄·ΝΟΥ·
-n	who-had-he	there	in-his- \ -field	a-

·Ε2Ο	ΕϤ·2[ΗΠ`	ΕϤ·]Ο	Ν̄·ΑΤ·CΟΟΥΝ`	ΕΡΟ·Ϥ	ΑΥ-
-treasure	()hiding,	he-being	not-knowing	about-him; >	an-

-ω	Μ̄[ΜΝ̄Ν̄CΑ·Τ]ΡΕϤ·ΜΟΥ	ΑϤ·ΚΑΑ·Ϥ	Μ̄·ΠΕϤ·`
-d	after-his-death,	he-left-him	to-his-

[·ϢΗΡΕ	ΝΕ·Π]ϢΗΡΕ	·CΟΟΥΝ	ΑΝ`	ΑϤ·ϪΙ·`
-son.	The-son	knew	not.	He-took-

·Τ·CωϣΕ	ΕΤ·Μ̄·ΜΑΥ	ΑϤ·ΤΑΑ·[C ΕΒΟλ ΑΥω ΠΕΝ]-
-the-field	which-was-there;	he-gave-her away, > and whoev-

·ΤΑ2·ΤΟΟΥ·C ΑϤ·ΕΙ ΕϤ·CΚΑΕΙ Α[Ϥ·2Ε] Α·Π·Ε2Ο ΑϤ·
-er-bought-her, he-came ()plowing; he-fell on-the-treasure. Did-he·

·ΑΡΧΕΙ	Ν̄·†·2ΟΜΤ`	Ε·Τ·ΜΗCΕ	Ν̄[·ΝΕΤ]·Ϥ·ΟΥΟϣ·ΟΥ
-begin	to-give-money	(at-interest)	to-those-he-loves().

Jesus said, "The kingdom is like a man who had a [hidden] treasure in his field without knowing it. And [after] he died, he left it to his [son]. The son [did] not know (about the treasure). He inherited the field and sold [it]. And the one who bought it went plowing and [found] the treasure. He began to lend money at interest to whomever he wished."

INTERPRETATION:

The passage is both analogous to and expands on the passage of **Matthew 13:44.**

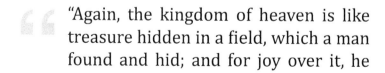

> "Again, the kingdom of heaven is like treasure hidden in a field, which a man found and hid; and for joy over it, he

goes and sells all that he has and buys that field."

It also agrees with the idea expressed in Luke 19:12-24 about the distribution of the mines, which the faithful traded to multiply them.

110

ΠΕΧΕ·ῙC̄	ΧΕ	ΠΕΝΤΑϩ·6ΙΝΕ	[Μ̄·]Π·ΚΟCΜΟC
Said Jesus	this:	Whoever-has-found	the-world
Ν̄ϥ·Ρ̄·ΡΜ̄·ΜΑΟ		ΜΑΡΕϥ·ΑΡΝΑ	Μ̄·Π·ΚΟCΜΟC
&()-become-rich,		let-him-abdicate	from-the-world.

Jesus said, "Whoever finds the world and becomes rich, let him renounce the world."

INTERPRETATION:

The passage may explain the moment Jesus asks the rich man to forsake all he has to be perfect in Matthew 19:16-26.

Matthew 19:21-22
"Jesus said to him, 'If you want to be perfect, go, sell what you have and give to the poor, and you will have treasure in heaven; and come, follow Me." But when the young man heard that saying, he left sorrowful, for he had great possessions."

The riches of the system can be a deadly hook for those who find them because they get caught up in the splendor, never wanting to let go.

111

ΠΕΧΕ·ĪC ΧΕ   Μ·ΠΗΥΕ   ·ΝΑ·6ωλ` ΑΥω   Π·ΚΑ2
Said Jesus this: The-heavens will-be-rolled-up, and the-earth,
Μ·ΠΕΤΝ·ΜΤΟ   ΕΒΟλ` ΑΥω ΠΕΤ·ΟΝ2 ΕΒΟλ 2Ν·
in-your(pl)-presence ( ) ;   > and   he-who-lives   out   of-
·ΠΕΤ·ΟΝ2 Ϥ·ΝΑ·ΝΑΥ ΑΝ Ε·ΜΟΥ   ΟΥΧ·2ΟΤΙ Ε·ĪC
-he-who-lives, he-will-look not on-death; >   because Jesus
·Χω Μ·ΜΟ·C ΧΕ ΠΕΤΑ·2Ε   ΕΡΟ·Ϥ` ΟΥΑΑ·Ϥ Π·ΚΟC-
-speaks of-it   this- whoever-falls upon-it himself,   the-wo-
-ΜΟC ·Μ̄ΠϢΑ Μ̄·ΜΟ·Ϥ` ΑΝ
-rld   be-worthy of-him   not.

Jesus said, "The heavens and the earth will be rolled up in your presence. And the one who lives from the living one will not see death." Does not Jesus say, "Whoever finds himself is superior to the world"?

INTERPRETATION:

The first part that speaks of the change of heaven and earth is explained in **Revelation 6:14.**

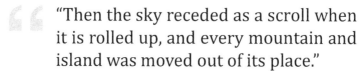

> "Then the sky receded as a scroll when it is rolled up, and every mountain and island was moved out of its place."

It provides the basis for interpreting the rest of the passage.

In the era of Christ, when heaven and earth were transformed, we can find ourselves in Him, or as Paul states, "I shall know as I was known."

1 Corinthians 13:12
"For now, we see in a mirror, dimly, but then face to face. Now I know in part, but then I shall know just as I also am known."

If we find ourselves in Him, it is because we have lost our life within this world's system.

Matthew 16:25
"For whoever desires to save his life will lose it, but whoever loses his life for My sake will find it."

112 ——————————

				ΠΕΧΕ·ΙC	ΧΕ	ΟΥΟΕΙ
-rld	be-worthy	of-him	not.	Said Jesus	this:	Woe
Ν·Τ·CΑΡΞ`	ΤΑΕΙ	ΕΤ·ΟϢΕ	Ν·Τ·ΦΥΧΗ			ΟΥΟΕΙ
on-the-flesh,	the-one	which-depends	on-the-soul;	(_)	>	Woe
Ν·Τ·ΦΥΧΗ	ΤΑΕΙ	ΕΤ·ΟϢΕ	Ν·Τ·CΑΡΞ			
on-the-soul,	the-one	which-depends	on-the-flesh.			

Jesus said, "Woe to the flesh that depends on the soul; woe to the soul that depends on the flesh."

Once again, this passage is analogous to Jeremiah 17:4-5 Jeremiah 17:4-5, which describes the judgment of apostate Judah, fulfilled in the year 70 AD.

Moreover, as we have seen above, it is a warning not to place our faith in the human system.

 Jeremiah 17:4-5

> "And you, even yourself, shall let go of your heritage which I gave you; and I will cause you to serve your enemies in the land which you do not know; for you have kindled a fire in My anger which shall burn forever." Thus says the Lord: 'Cursed is the man who trusts in man and makes flesh his strength, whose heart departs from the Lord.'

113

ⲡⲉϫⲁ·ⲩ
Said-they

ⲛⲁ·ϥ ⲛ̄ϭⲓ·ⲛⲉϥ·ⲙⲁⲑⲏⲧⲏⲥ ϫⲉ ⲧ·ⲙⲛ̄ⲧⲉⲣⲟ
to-him, viz-his-disciples, this: The-kingdom,

ⲉⲥ·ⲛ̄ⲛⲏⲩ ⲛ̄·ⲁϣ ⲛ̄·ϩⲟⲟⲩ ⲉⲥ·ⲛ̄ⲛⲏⲩ ⲁⲛ ϩⲛ̄·ⲟⲩ·
she-is-coming on-which day? > She-is-coming not in-a-

·ϭⲱϣⲧ` ⲉⲃⲟⲗ` ⲉⲩ·ⲛⲁ·ϫⲟ·ⲟⲥ ⲁⲛ ϫⲉ ⲉⲓⲥ·ϩⲏⲏ-
-look outward; >they-will-be-speaking not this- " Beho-

-ⲧⲉ ⲙ̄·ⲡⲓ·ⲥⲁ ⲏ ⲉⲓⲥ·ϩⲏⲏⲧⲉ ⲧⲏ ⲁⲗⲗⲁ ⲧ·ⲙⲛ̄ⲧⲉⲣⲟ
-ld, that-side" or "Behold, that-one"; > Rather, the-kingdom

ⲙ̄·ⲡ·ⲉⲓⲱⲧ` ⲉⲥ·ⲡⲟⲣϣ` ⲉⲃⲟⲗ ϩⲓϫⲙ̄·ⲡ·ⲕⲁϩ ⲁⲩⲱ
of-the-father, she-is-spreading out upon-the-earth, and

ⲣ̄·ⲣⲱⲙⲉ ·ⲛⲁⲩ ⲁⲛ ⲉⲣⲟ·ⲥ ⲡⲉϫⲉ·ⲥⲓⲙⲱⲛ·ⲡⲉⲧⲣⲟⲥ
men look not upon-her. >

His disciples said to him, "When will the kingdom come?" <Jesus said,> "It will not come by waiting for it. It will not be a matter of saying 'here it is' or 'there it is.' Rather, the kingdom of the father is spread out upon the earth, and men do not see it."

INTERPRETATION:

The verse is analogous to

> **Luke 17:20-21**
>
> "Now when He was asked by the Pharisees when the kingdom of God would come, He answered them and said, 'The kingdom of God does not come with observation; nor will they say, See here! or See there! For indeed, the kingdom of God is within you.'"

114

ΠΕΧΕ·ϹΙΜΩΝ·ΠΕΤΡΟϹ
>　　　　 Said-Simon-Peter

ΝΑ·Υ　ΧΕ　ΜΑΡΕ·ΜΑΡΙ2ΑΜ　·ΕΙ　ΕΒΟΛ　Ν·2ΗΤ·Ν
to-them　this:　Let-Mariam　come　out　from-us,

ΧΕ　Ν·Ϲ2ΙΟΜΕ　·ΜΠΩΑ　ΑΝ`　Μ·Π·ΩΝ2　ΠΕΧΕ·ΙϹ
for　(the)women　be-worthy　not　of(The)Life.　Said Jesus

ΧΕ　ΕΙϹ·2ΗΗΤΕ　ΑΝΟ·Κ`　†·ΝΑ·ϹΩΚ`　Μ·ΜΟ·Ϲ　ΧΕ-
this:　Behold,　I,　()will-lead　her,　so-

-ΚΑΑϹ　Ε·ΕΙ·ΝΑ·Α·Ϲ　Ν·2ΟΟΥΤ`　ΩΙΝΑ　Ϲ·ΝΑ·ΩΩ-
-that　I-might-make-her　male,　so　she-might-come-to-

-ΠΕ　2Ω·ΩϹ　Ν·ΟΥ·ΠΝΑ　ΕϤ·ΟΝ2　ΕϤ·ΕΙΝΕ　Μ·
-be　also-her(self)　a-spirit　()living,　()resembling　-

·ΜΩ·ΤΝ　Ν·2ΟΟΥΤ`　ΧΕ　Ϲ2ΙΜΕ　·ΝΙΜ`　ΕϹ·ΝΑ·Α·Ϲ
-you(pl)　male(s),　>　for　woman　-any　()making-her(self)

Ν·2ΟΟΥΤ`　Ϲ·ΝΑ·ΒΩΚ`　Ε2ΟΥΝ　Ε·Τ·ΜΝΤΕΡΟ·
male,　she-will-go　in　to-the-kingdom-

·Ν·Μ·ΠΗΥΕ
of(the)heaven(s).

Simon Peter said to them, "Let Mary leave us, for women are not worthy of life." Jesus said, "I myself shall lead her in order to make her male, so that she too may become a living spirit resembling you males. For every woman who will make herself male will enter the kingdom of heaven."

INTERPRETATION:

This last statement should not be interpreted without first taking into account two factors:

First, the line of the speech of Jesus' sayings described by Matthew warns more than once that the Kingdom implies the oneness of all things, arriving at an equality or equivalence as it was initially. That is to say that both men and women enter and become one in the last Adam.

That is why it says in another passage of this gospel:

> "Jesus said to them, "When you make the two one, and when you make the inside like the outside and the outside like the inside, and the above like the below, and when you make the male and the female one and the same, so that the male not be male nor the female," but they are one spirit in Him."

The same thing is emphasized in Sayings 106 and 48.

> "Jesus said, 'When you make the two one, you will become the sons of man, and when you say, 'Mountain, move away,' it will move away."

In the second place, Jesus speaks within a historical context, where inequalities were extreme between men and women.

Women were always regarded by the Hebrew culture as inferior, even compared to dogs. Therefore, they would always have a mindset of inferiority and even servitude.

But not so the service by choice as it corresponds to faith, but that which comes from a debased heart.

So, we believe that in the statement, he did not mean that he would change women anatomically into men, but that he wanted to change their mindset so that they would stop being constrained by the limited understanding of being a woman at that day in time and realize that they are capable of receiving from God the same spiritual privileges and authority.

As the Apostle Paul also taught:

Galatians 3:27-28
"For as many of you as were baptized into Christ have put on Christ. There is neither Jew nor Greek; there is neither slave nor free, there is neither male nor female; for you are all one in Christ Jesus."

And he further adds:

1 Corinthians 16:13
"Watch, stand fast in the faith, be brave, be strong."

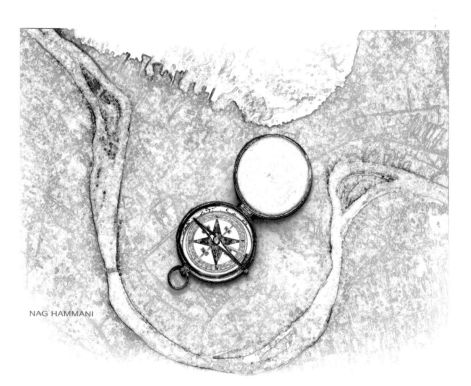

NAG HAMMANI

THE GOSPEL
THO^MAS

OF

APOCRYPHAL WITH COPTIC INTERLINEAR

COMMENTED BY: *Ana Méndez Ferrell, Simón Aquino,*
Ana Louceiro Plattner & Lorenza Méndez

VOICE OF THE LIGHT
MINISTRIES

We invite you to watch our online video series

www.voiceofthelight.com

If you enjoyed this book, we also recommend

The End of An Era
Rediscovering a Hidden History

Ignoring history causes us to fall into serious interpretation errors regarding "End of the World" prophecies. Jesus and the apostles used the word "aion" when they referred to the end of "an era" and not the word "Kosmos", which refers to "the world". The Jewish Historian, Flavius Josephus lived in the first century throughout the end of the Old Testament Jewish age and he described what took place in great detail in his books, "The Wars of the Jews."

In this book, Ana Méndez Ferrell makes a stunning compilation and summary of these very valuable historical writings, joining segments where we can clearly appreciate the fulfillment of all prophecies concerning the end. This book is very revealing and graphic. You will read about the signs seen in the sky and in the Temple as well as the horrors that occurred until the final destruction of old Israel.

Available on Amazon and our online store

www.voiceofthelight.com

Watch us on **Frequencies of Glory TV** and **YouTube**
Follow us on **Facebook**, **Instagram** and **Twitter**

www.frequenciesofglorytv.com
www.youtube.com/VoiceoftheLight

https://m.facebook.com/AnaMendezFerrellPaginaOficial
www.instagram.com/emerson.ferrell
www.twitter.com/MendezFerrell

Contact us today!

Voice of The Light Ministries
P.O. Box 3418
Ponte Vedra, FL. 32004
USA
904-834-2447

www.voiceofthelight.com

Printed in Poland
by Amazon Fulfillment
Poland Sp. z o.o., Wrocław

24049120R00101